Southern Living. GARDEN GUIDE

Houseplants

Series Editor: Lois Trigg Chaplin

Text by Kathleen English

Oxmoor House.

Contents

Library of Congress Catalog Number: 96-67716
ISBN: 0-8487-2244-2
Manufactured in the United States of America
First Printing 1996

Editor-in-Chief: Nancy Fitzpatrick Wyatt
Editorial Director, Special Interest Publications:
Ann H. Harvey
Senior Editor, Editorial Services: Olivia Kindig Wells
Art Director: James Boone

Southern Living Garden Guide HOUSEPLANTS

Series Editor: Lois Trigg Chaplin
Assistant Editor: Kelly Hooper Troiano
Copy Editors: Anne S. Dickson, Virginia Gilbert Loftin
Editorial Assistant: Allison D. Ingram
Garden Editor, *Southern Living*: Linda C. Askey
Indexer: Katharine R. Wiencke
Concept Designer: Eleanor Cameron
Designer: Carol Loria
Senior Photographer, *Southern Living*: Van Chaplin
Production and Distribution Director: Phillip Lee
Associate Production Manager: Vanessa C. Richardson
Production Coordinator: Marianne Jordan Wilson
Production Assistant: Valerie L. Heard

Our appreciation to the staff of *Southern Living*
magazine for their contributions to this book.

Dwarf Schefflera

Left: *Sansevieria*

Cover: *Gloxinia*
Frontispiece: *Arrowhead Vine*

Crossandra

Houseplants Primer

Houseplants are architecture and accent, color and expression, collectible and fashion statements.

Whether a green foliage plant or a plant with flowers, houseplants bring life and excitement to indoor decor.

Houseplants come into our lives in a variety of ways. They commemorate life's passages: birthdays and graduations, weddings and promotions, sickness and loss. Add to those the plants handed down, passed along, or picked up along the way, and you have a collection as rich as a photo album, documenting the joy of sharing living space with living beauty.

Houseplants often are the training ground of many gardeners-to-be. Before there is earth to turn and plant, there is a windowsill. First apartments often display the early experiments, and moving day reveals the winners and losers. It may be that a palm or philodendron from those early days is still part of your family.

Bringing plants inside links the lives we lead in homes and offices to the world outside. Collectors have always adapted eye-catching specimens from the wild to life indoors, vastly expanding the range of plants to be enjoyed in the home.

Large trees such as schefflera and weeping fig have been joined by more recent favorites such as ficus Alii and lady palm. With variegations, braided trunks, and companion underplantings, these plants bring a fresh approach to indoor decorating. Even plants traditionally grown outdoors such as azaleas and chrysanthemums now provide brief and seasonal interior color.

New hybrids and better understanding of cultural needs put orchids and other exotics within reach of amateur gardeners. Citrus trees not only yield luscious fruit, but they also fill the air with fragrance. And plant breeders keep improving familiar friends like spathiphyllum and Chinese evergreen.

Regardless of the plants you choose to bring into your home and share with others, these pages will be your guide to keeping them healthy and beautiful and will show you new ways to enjoy them year-round.

This miniature amaryllis has delicate flowers that will appear every year.

CONSIDER YOUR STYLE

Style is one of the most elusive components of decorating. In today's homes, even rooms done in a period style will blend in different elements from other periods. For example, while a fern on a stand represents Victorian or Early American style, ferns can also be used to create other decors.

A plant might be selected to suggest an easily recognizable style—such as the fern on a stand—but it is also chosen for the way it complements or contrasts with other elements in a room. If you notice plants in a decor, you may find yourself consistently responding to certain overall effects.

Palms and ferns can bring a breath of summer to a sunporch. Ribbon and ivy wreaths can echo Easter celebrations. Crotons can repeat autumn color visible through windows. And a grouping of forced bulbs can brighten winter blues. Just as you might switch slipcovers, pillows, and window treatments to create a seasonal transformation, you can rearrange plants to add to the effect.

Decorating with Plants Indoors

Houseplants often are overlooked or underused when it comes time to add personal touches to a room's decor.

Houseplants invite experimentation. While digging and moving garden plants to get the best effect can be challenging, you can easily rearrange all but the largest houseplants to suit your changing tastes and needs. As long as you keep in mind the plant's need for light and moisture, you are safe in testing new arrangements.

And because they are so portable, plants deserve the same consideration given to rugs, lamps, and accessories.

Plants as Elements of Interior Design

Plants and flowers give rooms vitality. They provide color, texture, height, and pattern. Large houseplants can provide a screen for privacy, form a background, visually balance large pieces of furniture,

The ficus Alii tree in the corner provides height and mass the way a tall piece of furniture might. Bromeliads around its base and the succulents planted in an earthenware bowl add exotic accents.

direct traffic from one space to another, or serve as sculptural accents. Medium-sized plants can fill empty spots beside chairs and tables and add dimension when grouped with larger plants. These same plants when placed on stands can take the place of larger plants.

The natural form of a plant suggests ways to use it. For example, the spreading branches of weeping fig make an excellent soft screen between areas of a room or can fill an empty corner with its foliage. In contrast, the slender, upright forms of corn plant or Madagascar dragon tree work better as a sculptural accent against a blank wall.

A showy small plant can be displayed on a tabletop by itself or it can be grouped with other plants in arrangements. Trailing plants can fill out the base around larger trees, add a graceful note to hanging baskets, or perch atop tall pieces of furniture where their cascading form is shown to advantage.

Groupings of large plants in front of windows add privacy and shade while blending with the greenery outside. Medium-sized plants on a table can do the same. In either case, the effect is distinctly different from that of draperies, shades, or shutters.

Sometimes a room arrangement needs more mass and a lower form to balance it. Spathiphyllum, anthurium, Chinese evergreen, and philodendron are some of the houseplants that can work in these situations.

Smaller plants can add detail. Just as books and figurines are arranged on furniture to provide interest, an African violet or a succulent dish garden will also add personality to a room. Use small plants where they can be admired up close, such as on bedside tables, shelves, or in the center of a dining or breakfast room table.

The striking pattern on the leaves of this begonia make it a good choice for a simple background.

Matching Houseplants to the Decor

The principles that apply to choosing furnishings also apply to choosing plants as decorating accents. Some choices seem obvious. A Southwestern-style home, for example, would not be complete without a cactus or two. Other interiors, especially eclectic styles, offer more room for mixing and matching.

Consider basic elements—color, form, and size—and then narrow your choices. Choose plants that meet your decorating needs and can thrive under the care and conditions you provide.

This artful arrangement of an amaryllis, a Rieger begonia, daisy mums, and an African violet echoes the colors and patterns of the fabrics used in this room.

Color

With indoor plants, color comes into play in many ways. The most obvious variations are among flowering plants, but foliage color and pattern are important, too. Even plants with solid green leaves have qualities that make them more suitable for some uses than others.

A flowering plant can complement colors in carpet and upholstery. It can blend into an overall color scheme or provide contrast, such as when a bright red begonia is placed in a room decorated in neutral tones. If a plant's flowers have a patterned foliage, this mosaic of color must be used carefully. For example, a blazing sword bromeliad, with its dramatic red flower and banded foliage, would be dizzying in front of red Chinese-patterned wallpaper. Placed in the center of a room or against a contrasting solid color, it provides drama.

Many foliage plants, such as calathea, croton, and begonia, offer color in the form of patterned leaves, which makes them a better choice than seasonally blooming plants for year-round color and texture. Plants with variegated leaves marked by white or silver can be used to lighten dark spots, just as deep green and burgundy foliage can add depth and weight to an empty space.

Consider the varying shades of green in foliage plants. Chartreuse creates a bright, warm effect, while blue-toned foliage is psychologically cooler. Which color you choose depends on whether you want a neutral or dramatic effect.

Form

Just like their outdoor counterparts, indoor plants come in a wide array of forms and textures. They can be dense or airy, upright or arching, finely textured or bold. Common growth habits include mounding, arching, clumping, or branching. Many popular smaller plants, like primula, grow in rosettes.

For boldness, consider plants with arching straplike foliage such as clivia and bromeliad. Ivy or trailing plants can provide softness, while the upright spiking sansevieria creates definition.

Use the plant's texture as a design tool. For example, if you want the illusion of distance in a room, choose a plant with smaller leaves, such as weeping fig. To bring a distant spot visually closer, use a plant with large leaves, such as fiddle-leaf fig or Black Cardinal philodendron.

Size

Because plants are living, growing things, they can be more difficult than a floor lamp or vase to fit into a decorating scheme. The small schefflera that is perfect beside a library table one year may be too large the next year. Just as you need to know a tree or shrub's ultimate size before you plant it, you need to know how large and fast an indoor plant will grow. The exception is with seasonal plants, such as poinsettia and forced azalea.

In some cases, as with a large schefflera, you can prune plants to maintain their form and size. Other plants, such as bird-of-paradise, which can reach 10 feet or more in optimal conditions, might be more difficult to control and so require careful placement.

Plants that tolerate lower light can sometimes be cajoled into growing more slowly if you place them in a dimmer spot and gradually limit their water and fertilizer until they acclimate. Before attempting this approach, check with your nursery to be sure your selection will survive under these conditions.

Consider a plant's scale to other objects in the room and also to people. The drooping foliage of a large plant can be unsettling if you find yourself sitting beneath it. A small plant beside a large armoire can be so dwarfed that you scarcely notice it. A bushy plant on a coffee table can obstruct vision. Large plants near stairways or doors can hinder traffic flow.

The arching flower stalks of a phalaenopsis orchid are a simple but dramatic accent in this grouping.

A Rieger begonia tucked into a basket makes a lovely centerpiece. Its scale is appropriate to the table and will not block vision.

Grouping Houseplants

Just as you position plants outside to flow together into a cohesive design, you need to group your indoor plants to maximize their effect. A collection of primula beside a chair can give the feel of a garden brought indoors. A tall plant with a mass of foliage at the top might appear more balanced with medium-sized plants grouped around its base. And a special star, such as amaryllis, might deserve to stand alone.

Cascades of curly-leaf ivy balance the arching bands of bromeliad foliage.

When grouping houseplants, think of how each can be shown to best advantage and complement its neighbors. For example, use a green bushing plant behind smaller variegated plants, so that the field of solid color will highlight the patterned foliage. Group staggered heights of plants to frame a seating area.

Repetition can also be effective. Traditional arrangements rely on symmetry, such as placing two medium or large plants of equal size on each side of a window. A few small plants of the same size create a band of foliage or flowers on a mantel or dining table.

You can draw attention to an area by using plants of the same size at different heights or dissimilar plants at the same height. Diagonal lines lead the eye to a piece of artwork on the wall, a window with a lovely view, or a treasured piece of furniture.

While you will not want to group every plant in the home with others, artful arrangements often add more impact to a room and show the plants to better advantage.

Displaying Plants Indoors

Style often lies in the details: how the plants are displayed, what sort of containers they are in, and how they are lighted. Since plants are three-dimensional objects, integrate them into a room as if they were a piece of sculpture.

Placing Houseplants

When you display plants, consider their base: a stand, chest, or stack of books. Elevating plants offers two advantages: It allows you to use an element that coordinates with your overall room design, and it puts the plants in a better position to get the light and air circulation they need.

Plant stands and pedestals come in a wide array of styles, including handcarved rosewood stands, wooden and plaster columns, and mirrored pedestals. A wall bracket is a good way to display a cascading plant when you want a slightly more formal look than a hanging basket would provide.

An alternative to the traditional method for displaying ferns, this wall bracket places the fern at the exact height that will best balance other furnishings in the room.

If you have small plants, shelves or étagères placed near windows allow you to mix textures by arranging foliage or flowering plants alongside other objects such as figurines, boxes, or pottery. Footed oriental stands come in a range of sizes and can be an elegant way to turn a plant on a tabletop into a focal point.

If your style is more casual, use old trunks, butter churns, and stools to elevate larger plants. For smaller plants that need to be near windows, bring a country-style window box inside. You can mount it on the wall just below the window or place it on legs. You can also use a low table that is chosen to blend with any style.

Selecting Containers

Containers are the easiest way to make a humble plant shine. Selecting the right one calls for many of the same principles used in your choice of display.

The standard terra-cotta pot is a design workhorse. It serves well in almost any setting, is inexpensive, and is a healthy choice for most plants. The fashion of antiquing terra-cotta pots—either by allowing them to weather and collect algae and moss outdoors or by painting them to simulate an aged appearance—creates containers that are popularly used even in formal interiors.

One way to make a quick transformation is to attach florist's sheet moss with hot glue to the sides of a pot and secure the moss with a few lengths of raffia. If you are handy with a paintbrush and other crafter's tools, you can decorate a terra-cotta pot to match any decor.

Above and right: *To dress a simple clay pot, simply wrap the pot in sheet moss. Hold it in place with raffia string or hot glue.*

Some containers, such as glazed pots with attached saucers, have drainage holes; others are designed to hold plants potted in plastic pots. These cachepots come in a range of styles from oriental to modern. You can find them to suit any taste and budget.

Try creating containers from everyday items in the home by placing a plastic saucer inside them. Baskets are most commonly used this way, but a trip to the attic or basement might turn up some other intriguing items. Old-fashioned suitcases, boxes with lids that prop open, antique kitchen tins, or even an old boot are just a few of

A picnic basket containing an amaryllis gives extra style to a straightforward arrangement.

the possibilities. And do not overlook your household decorative items when you are considering your options. A silver wine bucket, an earthenware pitcher, or china cups and bowls can be wonderful ways to display your plants for parties and special occasions.

A Dutch porcelain bowl is perfect for these emerging paperwhites. A few cut daffodils from the garden are added for surprise.

*Light cast from the
nearby table lamp
highlights the orchid's
delicate color.*

Accenting with Light

Where you put your plants depends on the type light they need, but
light has another role to play in displaying plants: it can add to their
decorative effect. The most obvious example is placing a small flowering plant beside a table lamp where the lamp's warm, incandescent
glow can highlight the color of the flowers.

For drama at night, position a canister or directional uplight
beneath large plants, such as palm, weeping fig, or saddle-leaf
philodendron. The light will not only highlight foliage tones but will
also cast a patterned shadow on ceilings and walls. Uplights used
behind plants on pedestals create similarly striking effects. Specialty
stores and catalogs also offer waterproof halogen lights on spikes that
are designed to be inserted in soil.

If you have track lights or adjustable inset lights in your ceiling, use them to focus on a tree or grouping of plants as you would
spotlight artwork. This is especially effective in entryways and halls.

Special Effects

Flowering and foliage plants lend themselves to combinations that rival the most elaborate florist's creations.

By paying attention to the individual needs of plants and learning a few tricks of the trade, you can create stunning live arrangements that will enhance your home each season.

Creating Live Arrangements

Used as centerpieces, party decorations, or table accessories, live arrangements offer a fresh way to decorate. Depending on care, an arrangement will stay fresh from a few weeks to several months, possibly even a year. Because they endure, living arrangements are more practical than cut flowers. In many cases, the cost is the same.

Living arrangements are good choices to brighten up vacation homes, and they are perfect for the holidays because they remain

This opulent arrangement uses an abundance of plants and even sprigs of wild grasses to get the right balance of color, height, and texture.

This combination of foliage and flowering plants looks as if a part of the garden glimpsed beyond has come indoors.

fresh through several parties. There is no water to spill, making them ideal for picnics or tailgate parties. And nothing could be better to take to a hospital patient than an arrangement that lasts long enough to be enjoyed in good health.

Tabletop Combinations

The principles that apply to cut flower arranging apply to living arrangements, too. Treat the design like a miniature garden and work with a combination of foliage and flowering plants. Upright and trailing forms are a reminder of trees and vines growing outdoors.

A small arrangement may hold as few as three plants. In that case, pick two with color and another that is green; for example, group together a chrysanthemum, violet, and fern. Larger arrangements can have more variety and allow you room to experiment.

Foliage provides texture and serves as a foil for the flowers. Good choices include maidenhair, Dallas, and Boston ferns as well as creeping fig and ivy. Avoid using more than one variegated foliage plant in an arrangement.

By establishing a good foundation of green, you can keep an arrangement going for a full year by changing flowers seasonally. Forced bulbs, including paperwhites, hyacinths, and tulips are good choices for winter and spring. After that, turn to cyclamen and primula for color. Summer offers annual bedding plants such as zinnias or petunias.

Small figurines and other decorative touches can add detail and interest to large-scale arrangements.

Special Effects

Other good choices for color include streptocarpus, African violet, crossandra, begonia, kalanchoe, caladium, orchid, and azalea. If you use a plant like an orchid or a crossandra that has exacting cultural requirements, relocate it into the arrangement for a few days or a special occasion, and then return it to its regular growing location.

A phalaenopsis orchid rises above a mass of texture and color provided by crossandra, maidenhair fern, zebra grass, and ivy.

Tabletop Containers

The choices of containers can be as creative as the arrangement. For special occasions, you can use a china serving piece, a silver bowl, or an item that suggests the theme of a celebration, such as a small sleigh during Christmas. For more permanent arrangements, choose a basket or something that will provide a neutral foundation.

If you choose the right container for an arrangement of compatible plants and then prepare it properly, watering will be easier. The idea is to be able to water the entire group of plants without having to take the group apart.

Ceramic containers. A ceramic container without a drainage hole is moisture-proof, so you do not have to worry about leaks on floors or furniture. On the other hand, be cautious not to water so much that the container fills up and drowns your plants. Choose a pot with a diameter one or two sizes larger than the host plant's pot to give the additional plants room to settle.

You can also use a large container that requires several plants to fill it up. Leave plants in individual pots, and add height by placing plants on blocks of plastic foam or overturned pots.

Baskets. If you use a basket, line it with a heavy-duty plastic garbage bag to contain the water that will drain from the pots. Put one or two plastic saucers in the bottom, and then set the main plant within the basket, still in its container. Trim the excess plastic around the upper edge of the basket, and set additional potted plants in place.

If the basket is small, slip the plants out of their pots, shake the excess soil from the roots, set them in place, and then fill the spaces between plants with potting soil. Unlike plants in pots with drainage holes, these arrangements need to be watered carefully. Give them enough, but not so much that they sit in a puddle.

Whichever method you use, conceal the mechanics by covering the surface with sphagnum or Spanish moss. Purchased moss is best, since materials you gather from nature are often home to insects.

Plants in pots allow you to experiment with an arrangement and to change out plants as their flowers fade.

A plastic lining in this basket holds dwarf narcissus, grape hyacinths, and a small mum so they can be watered without damaging the buffet.

19

A bromeliad and grape ivy, still in their own pots, dress up the base of this ficus Alii.

Embellishing Houseplants

Your everyday houseplants also can benefit from creative combinations. Many of the techniques used to create living tabletop arrangements can be used to create the illusion of a miniature garden growing beneath an indoor tree. This concept is not as difficult to implement as it might seem. As with tabletop arrangements, plants do not have to grow in the same pot.

Putting Plants Together

The foundation of the design is a large plant, potted in a utilitarian plastic container and placed inside a basket or other decorative container. Smaller plants, still in their pots, rest on top of the soil of the larger plant. You just nestle together enough small plants to conceal their pots and leave them in place to water.

When matching plants, be sure that their water requirements are compatible. A weeping fig, for example, would drown in the amount of water it would take to keep a maidenhair fern healthy. Ivy and spathiphyllum are better companion plants.

Take advantage of the flexibility these arrangements offer by rotating in flowering plants for seasonal color: begonias for summer, poinsettias at Christmas, mums for fall. For special occasions, you can include more perishable color. In summer, you can use colorful bedding plants. Buy inexpensive packs of four or six flowering transplants, and tuck them into the trailing foliage. For a shot of color, buy flowers from the florist or gather them from your garden. Cut the stems the appropriate length, place them in water picks, and stick the picks into the soil.

You can also apply this design to smaller plants. The dominant plant can be a Kentia palm on a buffet or sideboard. Even a dwarf spathiphyllum becomes lush and full when supplemented in this fashion. Just select smaller plants to go beneath it, such as variegated English ivy, and be sure they trail over the edge to complement the more upright forms.

Small plants can also benefit from embellishment. Use cut flowers in water picks or small flowering transplants to add color to tabletop plants, ivy baskets, and topiaries.

Combining Plants

Maybe you like the look of taller plants combined with smaller ones in a single container but do not have the time to constantly adjust them. You can keep it simple by potting a few compatible plants together, such as a ficus tree with pothos planted at the base, or create a tabletop dish garden.

When choosing companion plants, be sure that they have the same requirements for light, water, humidity, fertilizer, and soil. For the base of a tree-sized plant, choose companions that will trail over the edge of the pot and that respond to an occasional snipping, such as golden pothos or creeping fig. Look for plants with a texture that will complement the foliage of the host plant. A different texture gives the taller houseplant more interest by cloaking the exposed soil.

You can also combine plants in an old-fashioned, but still popular, dish garden. The same compatibility principles apply to these smaller arrangements. Be sure to use a container with adequate drainage and a soil mix that is appropriate to the plants. Dish gardens are appropriately named because they often need to be tended like a garden. As plants grow, you may need to prune them or replace them. For low maintenance, a dish garden of slow-growing plants such as cacti or succulents is a better choice.

Choose plants with a variety of forms to create interest: columnar or upright for the rear of the arrangement, lower round or dense plants for mass, and trailing or spreading plants to form the foreground. Even with an all-foliage plant arrangement, you can introduce color and pattern with variegated selections.

PLANTS THAT MAKE GOOD COMPANIONS

These are a few combinations that work well. If you leave the companion plants in their pots, you can easily experiment with others.

Host	Companions
Corn plant	Creeping fig Golden pothos
Ficus Alii Fiddle-leaf fig Weeping fig	Ivy Wax plant Golden pothos
Madagascar dragon tree	Rex begonia Miniature English ivy Heart-leaf philodendron
Schefflera	Ivy Heart-leaf philodendron Golden pothos
Spathiphyllum	Creeping fig Wax plant

Getting Started

To successfully grow houseplants, first understand your home environment and then select healthy plants.

When you choose plants for the garden, you match them to the conditions you can provide: light levels, temperature ranges, and soil composition. Your home has varied conditions, too. By understanding how to evaluate your interior, you can take the guesswork out of matching plant to location.

Know the Environment

Most of the plants we bring into the home are natives of tropical regions, yet we grow them in heated and air-conditioned homes. Fortunately, many houseplants adapt well, and by understanding their needs, you can create environments in which they will thrive.

Light

Plants use light to create the energy that fuels growth and keeps them green and healthy. If there is too little light, regardless of what else you do, your plant will starve. Leaves will gradually fade, and the plant will become weak, spindly, and ugly as leaves drop. This is why it is important to know the amount of light each plant needs.

If the walls in a room are white or light, they will reflect light. Dark walls absorb it. Light intensity changes with the time of year and the angle of the sun. In winter, the sun is lower in the sky and tends to shine more directly into south-facing windows than it will a few months later when it is higher overhead.

In positioning houseplants, you may know to draw on the basics: south-facing windows receive the brightest light; northern windows, the dimmest; and east- and west-facing windows have amounts that fall somewhere in between. But there is more to judging light.

To judge the level of light in a specific location, try the paper test. Take a blank piece of white paper and position it near the plant's foliage level. Hold your hand a foot above the paper and look at the shadow your hand casts. A shadow with sharp edges indicates bright light. A hazier shadow means the site receives medium light, and a faint or absent shadow indicates low light. Plants generally need four to five hours of light each day. To develop an accurate picture of the suitability of any given site, use the paper test. Check a location at intervals during the brightest time of day, generally between 10 a.m. and 2 p.m., and at different times of the year.

The ultimate indicator of light is the plant itself. Watch it during the first few weeks for signs of too little or too much light.

By matching your plants to the right conditions, you can ensure lush growth and abundant flowering.

Look at the distance between leaves on old stems of the plant. These were formed in greenhouse conditions. If this space is longer on newer stems, the plant is receiving insufficient light.

In too little light, new leaves may also be small and pale. Variegated leaves often lose their characteristic markings. If the plant is close to the wall under a window, try moving it out a little to catch a broader band of light. If you place a plant close to a wall under a window, the band of light may pass over its foliage and provide only medium or low amounts of illumination. A plant that receives good light in winter might suffer in summer when trees leaf out and screen the sun's rays. If placing the plant further from the window does not work, you may need to move it to another window or provide it with artificial light.

In too much light, leaves may wilt, become yellow, or develop spots. Some plants drop leaves. If this is a problem, shift the plant closer to the window or screen the sunshine with a curtain during part of the day. If the problem persists, put it in another location.

In general, try to provide plants with the most light you can without stressing them. They will reward you with good growth, full foliage, and ample blooms.

Temperature and Air Flow

Most houseplants can accommodate typical indoor temperatures, preferring between 70 and 80 degrees during the day and 60 to 65 degrees at night. Flowering plants such as holiday cactus like cooler nights, between 50 and 60 degrees, especially to initiate flower bulbs. Keep these plants in the coolest rooms of the house in winter.

However, be particularly careful that plants near windows remain warm enough in winter. Do not allow foliage to touch glass, which conducts cold. Plants that are too hot or too cold may stop growing, and their leaves may turn yellow, wilt, curl, and drop. While many plants can withstand temperatures as low as 40 degrees for short periods of time, most houseplants are damaged by temperatures that are well above freezing.

Plants also require good air circulation to maintain their health. Stagnant air can lead to disease and encourage insect infestations. However, plants should not be placed in drafts. Cross currents of air can dry foliage and cause leaf drop. Keep plants away from foyers or other entries where cold air blows in.

Several plants are suitable to low light levels in the home. Here golden pothos and Chinese evergreen flank tall sansevieria.

PLANTS THAT TOLERATE LOW LIGHT

These plants can accommodate low light levels in the home. Just remember that low light does not mean no light.

Aspidistra
Chinese evergreen
Dracaena
Golden pothos
Heart-leaf philodendron
Sansevieria

How Large Will Plants Get?

Because light levels are lower indoors than outdoors, plants tend to be smaller when grown exclusively indoors. If you give plants only enough light to remain healthy, you can moderate their growth. If you want a plant to grow larger, move it outside in the summer, and give it plenty of water and fertilizer.

Many plants can be pruned to maintain a desired shape and size. Pinching back stem tips causes plants such as pothos, ivy, and Benjamin fig to put their energy into adding fullness instead of length or height. With a plant that grows in a clump, such as aspidistra, you can sometimes remove larger leaves to control height or divide it to form two or more smaller plants.

Matching plants to space can be tricky. This schefflera, which fills the corner, can be pruned to maintain its size. The corn plant beside the chair might need a new location when it gets taller.

Humidity

Many plants can tolerate the dry air produced by central heating and air conditioning, but they would be much more comfortable with more humidity. Some flowering plants, such as anthurium and crossandra, require high humidity to produce blooms. An inexpensive weather gauge will reveal your home's humidity level. Most plants are healthiest when the humidity is between 40 and 60 percent. However, most homes have humidity levels of 15 to 20 percent, especially if the air conditioner or heater is running continuously.

Plants release moisture through their leaves in a process called *transpiration*. When plants are in dry air, they lose water through transpiration more quickly than their roots can replace it. At levels less than 15 to 20 percent, plants may wilt or develop leaf edges and tips that wrinkle and turn brown. More sensitive plants might show signs of stress when levels fall into the 30 to 40 percent range.

You may be able to solve the problem by moving a susceptible plant to a room that is more humid, such as a bathroom, laundry room, or kitchen. Experiment with methods of adding moisture to the air. The bonus is that you also will benefit from the more moist air. (See page 26 for more about raising the humidity indoors.)

How To Select Healthy Plants

Finding a healthy plant that is suited to your tastes, needs, and the environment in your home begins when you visit a plant shop. Inspect the likely candidates for their general condition and make a wise selection. Use care in introducing the plant to your home to ensure a smooth transition.

Match Your Expectations

It has happened to everyone at one time or another. You are in a store and something catches your eye. Before you know it, you are on your way home with your impulse buy. If that purchase is a plant, you may be setting yourself up for disappointment.

Some plants shoot up quickly; others grow at a snail's pace. Some plants are tolerant; others languish despite (or because of) your careful ministrations. Some plants will grow old with you gracefully, and others will not last long enough to be the centerpiece at a dinner party next week.

No matter how desirable a plant seems in the store, be sure it meets your requirements before you buy it. Think about ultimate size, both in height and in diameter. You can prune some plants to keep them in bounds, but are you really going to give a plant regular snippings? If not, opt for a plant that will not outgrow its space.

Be realistic about the care you are willing and able to provide. If your initial enthusiasm could yield to a demanding schedule or even absent-mindedness, choose a plant that will hang in there when your attention is elsewhere. The information contained in the profiles beginning on page 39 will help you identify some plants that will suit your needs.

Signs of Insects, Disease, or Stress

Inspect plants for healthy, abundant foliage that is free of insects, disease, or signs of stress. Plants that are leggy with few leaves have been grown in poor conditions. Pass by these and those with limp or yellow leaves. Foliage should begin at the bottom of the stems except in plants such as dracaena or dieffenbachia that naturally lose lower leaves as they mature.

Look for insects on the top and underside of leaves, along leaf veins, and at the junctures between leaves and stems. (See pages 124–125 for more about insects and their identification.)

Major signs of disease are discolored yellow, red, or brown spots or blotches on leaves; oozing from the leaves or stems; and green and yellow mosaic patterns on the leaves. Plants with root problems will be limp, as if they needed water, only they do not recover after watering. A few brown leaf tips are probably nothing to worry about; however, most leaves should be uniform in color, firm, and undamaged.

Plants can be a major investment, and it can pay to give your business to reputable shops and growers. No matter where you purchase your plants, it is a good idea to keep them segregated from your other plants for the first couple of weeks and watch them carefully. That way, if a problem reveals itself after you get the plants home, you can address it quickly and keep it from spreading.

Buy your houseplants from a reputable source and check them to be sure that they are healthy.

When you look for signs of insects, be especially careful inspecting plants such as begonias that have textured and patterned foliage.

Whether you have constructed a
lighting system for several
plants or are nourishing a single
specimen with a spotlight, use
an automatic timer to turn the
lights on and off on a regular
schedule.

*After orchids bloom, they should be
moved back under artificial lights.*

Ways To Improve Indoor Conditions

If you want to grow a plant that is particular about its environment, a
greenhouse is not the only choice. You can supplement natural light
with fluorescent or special incandescent lights. Other options include
raising humidity levels or increasing air circulation by opening a
window or using a fan.

Artificial Lighting

If your plants are located where they do not receive enough sunshine,
you can provide additional light with fluorescent lamps. Invest in
specially designed lighting systems for plants, such as spotlights to
highlight plants that are a permanent fixture in room decor. You can
create a spotlight with a two-bulb fixture suspended from the ceiling
or from a frame that holds the lights over the table. To get a good
range and intensity of light, use two 40-watt lamps, including a cool
white lamp and a warm white lamp or a grow-fluorescent lamp.

For houseplants that do not increase much in height, such as
African violet and orchid, mount the fixture so that it hangs 1 foot
above the tops of the plants. For plants that will grow taller, mount
the fixture so that it can be raised or lowered by using chains that slip
over eye hooks mounted on the ceiling or on a tall frame.

If fluorescent lights are the only source of light for plants,
leave them on for 16 to 18 hours a day. If the plants receive some natural light, experiment to achieve the right balance of the two. The
general rule is to turn on the lights for 12 hours each day. In either
case, be sure the time of day the lights are on coincides as closely as
possible with when plants would receive natural light.

Ambient Humidity

After light, providing enough humidity is probably the biggest hur-
dle to growing healthy plants indoors. If the air in your home is
extremely dry, you will need to raise the humidity around your plants
to keep them healthy.

The only sure way to significantly elevate moisture in the air is
to use a humidifier or cool-mist vaporizer in the room with the plants.
You can conceal small room humidifiers behind foliage or furniture.

Select Appropriate Containers

The pot you choose for a plant is important not only to its appearance but also to its health. With any pot, drainage is essential. If a container does not have a drainage hole, it should only be used for double potting—that is, holding a plant potted in another container.

This decorative ceramic cachepot is an attractive way to display a streptocarpus planted in a plastic pot with a drainage hole.

Material

Clay pots are the most common container used for houseplants. Since they are porous, water evaporates through the pot itself. Their weight also provides stability, especially for tall plants, such as a ficus tree, that could be toppled in a light container. Clay pots are harder to clean than nonporous containers, however, and can absorb chemicals, retain fertilizer salts, and even harbor disease. When you use old clay pots, make sure you first clean them thoroughly.

Plastic containers are inexpensive and useful both for double potting and for burying plants in soil outdoors during summer. They may not be sturdy enough to balance tall or top-heavy plants such as clivia and bromeliads. Glass, metal, wooden, and glazed pots offer other attractive alternatives but are usually more expensive than plastic. Self-watering containers made of plastic are convenient because they hold extra water in a reservoir, thus minimizing watering requirements.

Size

The size of a pot is important to the growth of the roots. If a container is too large, soil can remain too moist. In a container that is too small, there is not enough soil to hold water; roots can become dense and girdled. The plant will dry out too quickly because there is not enough soil to hold the moisture that it needs. Most plants should be potted in a container that measures one to two inches larger in diameter than the root ball; this should be large enough to support growth for one year.

Caring for Houseplants

Plants that receive the proper care reward you with lush foliage and colorful blooms.

Plants like this orchid that is potted and set in a cachepot can be moved to a sink for watering.

Once you choose a plant, the routine care begins. If you have made sure to match the plant to its surroundings, then watering, feeding, and other maintenance will be easy.

Watering

Watering plants seems simple enough. But most plant care problems stem from incorrect watering. Too much water is worse than too little, so it is important to water just enough to meet a plant's needs.

Consider the Water Itself

Most of the time, tap water is fine for houseplants. Extremely hard water with its high mineral content and alkaline pH can stress plants over time. Naturally soft water is best but not water that has been altered with most softeners. These can add harmful sodium. If you live in an area known for its hard water, use rain water periodically to minimize these problems.

Because tap water has high levels of chlorine, you need to fill your watering can and let it sit for 24 hours to allow the chlorine to evaporate. This will help prevent the browning of leaf tips and lets the water warm to room temperature. Cold water shocks roots and damages sensitive plants such as African violet.

Know How Often To Water

Watering is the single most important way to care for your plants, and improper watering is the quickest way to kill them. Soil that is too wet cannot hold sufficient air, so your plants may develop root rot or disease or may literally drown. In soil that is kept too dry, roots may die back, leaving plants constantly limp or wilted from stress.

A good general rule for most houseplants is to water thoroughly when the top inch of soil becomes dry. The best way to test this is by sticking your finger into the soil. With medium to small plants, you can also pick them up to check weight. After keeping plants for a while, you learn from experience if the pot is too light, which means it is too dry.

A plant's appearance tells you if you are watering too much, too little, or just enough. Dull, off-color foliage or brown-edged leaves signal too little water. Yellowing or rotting leaves tells you that a plant is getting too much water.

Wilting is the classic sign that a plant needs watering. But under certain conditions, it can mean that you have watered too much. If a well-watered plant begins wilting, it has been overwatered, and the soil does not have enough oxygen.

Several conditions can affect how often you need to water. Dry air, warm temperatures, and porous pots cause plants to lose water more quickly. You also need to increase watering in spring and summer when houseplants are growing new leaves and stems. Plants may need more water in bright, sunny rooms than in darker areas of the house. Of course, plants outdoors on a patio will need more water because they are more likely to put on new growth outdoors.

Know How To Water

There are two ways to water plants: from the top and submerged. Watering from the top is often the most convenient. Pour the water as evenly as possible around the base of the plant on all sides of the pot. Give plants enough water to cause a little excess to drain through the pot and collect in saucers. Drain any that remains in the saucer within a few hours of watering. Plants that are left standing in water can develop root rot.

Submerging a pot allows you to water from the bottom. Place pots in a tub, sink, bucket, or bowl holding an inch or two of water. Water will seep up through the drainage hole so that the soil draws up as much water as it can absorb. As with top watering, plants should not be left in water for more than a few hours.

This technique is especially useful for plants with sensitive foliage and a tendency to crown rot, such as African violets. It is also good for plants potted in a fast-draining medium like bark chips and for soil that has become too dry and has pulled away from the sides of the pot. In an extreme case of dried-out soil, submerge the entire container in enough water to just cover the top of the pot and leave it there until bubbles stop rising to the surface.

Fertilizing

Most houseplants do not require frequent, year-round doses of fertilizer. Since their light exposure is limited, they grow slowly or not at all. Light, regular feeding during spring and summer is usually sufficient to maintain good health. A few flowering plants such as African violets and orchids have higher needs, so check the specific recommendations of the plant you are trying to grow. Houseplants grown in sunrooms or other bright exposures will need regular feeding to support new growth.

SELF-WATERING CONTAINERS

Plants that must be kept constantly moist can benefit from being potted in a self-watering container. These work by wicking water from a reservoir into the plant's soil. Just make sure the reservoir remains full.

You can buy self-watering containers in a wide variety of styles, or make your own with clay pots. You need a wick, a saucer, and two containers of the same size and style with drainage holes. For the wick, cut a 6-inch length of synthetic yarn or string. Natural materials are unsuitable because they rot.

Put one end of the wick through the drainage hole into one of the containers, and then pot your plant. (You can use a sharp instrument to push one end of the wick through the drainage hole into the soil of an already potted plant.) Place the other container upside down in the saucer. Fill the saucer with water and position the plant on top, slipping the wick through the bottom container's exposed drainage hole and into the water reservoir.

This begonia appreciates the lift it gets from blossom booster fertilizers, which contain higher levels of phosphorus and potassium.

Clean the begonia's hairy leaves with a soft, dry paintbrush to remove accumulated dust and debris.

For most plants, a balanced, water-soluble, all-purpose fertilizer, such as a 20-20-20, works well. Never apply fertilizer to dry soil because this can cause the roots to burn. Water a dry plant thoroughly a few hours before feeding.

You can also use slow-release granules, pellets, or sticks. Just be sure to monitor how long it has been between applications to provide the proper level of nutrients. Each product is formulated to last a specific time, so check the label. Most plants do not need fertilizing in winter when growth slows or stops. In spring and summer, a good rule of thumb is to feed them every two to three weeks.

Flowering plants may require a fertilizer with a higher potassium content, often called blossom booster. Many manufacturers make fertilizers blended for flowering plants like African violets and orchids. When using one of these, follow directions carefully for best results.

Fertilizer can build up in soil over time, damaging roots. To prevent this, periodically ***leach***, or flush, the soil by pouring large amounts of water through it, washing it thoroughly. Leaching is especially important in plants that are usually watered by submersion.

Grooming

Be sure to routinely clean your houseplants. Dust can clog the pores of leaves, making it difficult for them to exchange air and transpire. For plants with shiny leaves, wipe the tops and bottoms with a damp cloth or paper towel. Hairy leaves such as those of an African violet or certain begonias can be gently brushed clean with a soft, dry paintbrush.

You can also periodically rinse all but hairy-leafed plants in the shower or under a hose. Wash them early in the day so that they have ample time to dry before sunset, and do not leave them standing in water. Rinsing rids the plant of dust and reduces spider mites.

If you like shiny leaves, use a commercial leaf shine product. Some plants, such as calatheas, are sensitive to these products, so before using one, be sure there is no caution about your plant in the directions for use.

To keep plants looking their best, shape them occasionally. Pinching the stem tips of branching plants produces more side shoots and leaves, so the plant becomes fuller. Pinching is especially useful in controlling vining plants like ivy, pothos, heart-leaf philodendron, wax plant, and creeping fig.

Larger, woody plants can also be pruned to improve their form. Always use sharp, clean clippers, and make cuts at the point on the stem where you want new growth to begin. Ficus trees respond well to this type of pruning. If a plant is spindly or badly formed, you can often cut it back severely to promote lush new growth.

If plants develop yellow leaves, remove them carefully so that you do not harm healthy stems. Cut off brown tips with scissors, being sure to follow the leaf's original shape with your cuts. Remove and discard any diseased parts, including leaves that have fallen on the soil surface.

Ivy responds so well to pinching that it is often trained along wire forms.

HOW LONG DO HOUSEPLANTS LIVE?

A few houseplants get passed down from generation to generation. Others are treated as seasonal items and are discarded within a few weeks. In general, most houseplants can live indefinitely if they receive the ideal care, but they are often replaced within two years because most homes do not provide ideal conditions.

Palms and ficus plants are prized for their longevity indoors provided they receive proper light, water, fertilization, and pest control. Other long-lived indoor plants include citrus, clivia, orchid, wax plant, and holiday cactus. These plants may live 10 years or more with good care. Many flowering plants are grown for brief, seasonal use and then discarded. Among these are florist's azaleas and mums, forced bulbs, cineraria, poinsettia, gloxinia, cyclamen, and primula.

Moving Plants Indoors and Out

If you like to treat your plants to the outdoors, these tricks help make the transition easy. Even plants that grow in bright light indoors will burn if moved directly into sunshine outdoors. Place all plants in full shade initially to allow them time to acclimate to the stronger light.

If you have plants that need consistently moist soil, dress the tops of the pots with mulch or bury pots in soil up to their rims to reduce evaporation. Be sure to twist them from time to time to keep roots from lodging through drainage holes.

Bring your plants inside before cool temperatures can harm them. First, prune any spindly or errant branches, removing any stems or leaves that are dead or diseased.

Repot those plants whose roots are growing out of drainage holes or coming to the surface of the soil. For others, repotting is best left until spring. (See page 33 for more about repotting.) If repotting is not necessary, be sure to clean the outer surfaces of your containers. After a summer outdoors, they may have to be scrubbed with a brush.

Next, clean the leaves by wiping them or rinsing them with a hose. Inspect leaves for any signs of insects and treat accordingly. Even if you do not find any evidence, consider spraying leaves with insecticidal soap in case insect eggs are present.

Once you bring plants indoors, locate them where they will receive as much natural light as possible. Plants you want to display in a lower light setting should be moved gradually into position to reduce shock.

Plants such as this fiddle-leaf fig enjoy spending the summer outdoors. But be sure to thoroughly clean any plant before bringing it inside for winter.

Basics of Repotting

As plants grow, you will need to move them to a larger pot with fresh soil. Repotting lets you refresh plants by making sure that they have enough soil to accommodate their roots, and that the soil is conditioned to hold nutrients and moisture. Even plants that do not grow much can benefit from repotting because their soil mix may begin to break down.

When To Repot a Plant

Recognizing when a plant needs repotting is a skill that comes with experience. Some plants, such as Chinese evergreen, clivia, aspidistra, sansevieria, and schefflera, prefer to be slightly rootbound. Clivia does not really produce spectacular blooms until the roots are crammed together in the pot.

With these few exceptions, most plants will signal the need for repotting. If you notice that they need more frequent drinks and that growth has slowed or stopped, you probably need to repot. However, if you want to slow your plant's growth, you can put a plant back into the container it was growing in. To do this, cut back roots enough so they are not crowded in the container. Snip off the outer edges of the root ball with sharp kitchen shears. Cut the top of the plant back by about 20 percent to compensate for the loss of roots. Then the plant is ready to repot in the same size container.

Do you want to encourage growth? Do not be misled into thinking a much bigger pot will boost growth. Plants perform better if you advance by only one pot size—an inch to an inch and a half larger—at a time.

Resist the temptation to repot a new plant right away. It will be going through enough adjustments in its first weeks without having to become established in a new container. If you do not like its pot, hide it in a cachepot or basket.

How To Repot

When repotting your houseplant, use a new pot or one you have used before. If you use an old clay pot, scrub it thoroughly, and sterilize it by soaking it for a couple of hours in a mixture of one part household bleach to nine parts water. This ensures that the pot does not harbor fungus spores or other diseases.

Repotting gives plants room to continue growing.

Plants that live for several years such as this begonia will need repotting every year or two.

This epiphytic orchid requires a coarse bark potting mix.

Cover the drainage hole with a piece of wire screen or a paper coffee filter to keep soil from washing through it. Fill the bottom of the pot with an inch or two of moist potting soil. (If the potting soil is dry, pour it into a bucket or wheelbarrow and moisten.) Now you are ready to remove the plant from its old container.

Plants with moist soil slip out more easily, so water the plant before removing it from its container. Gently lay the plant on its side if it is large or hold it sideways in your hand if it is small. Tap the pot to release the soil and pull the old container off while supporting the plant's stem. Pull on the container, not the plant, to prevent ripping the plant away from its roots. If roots are growing out of the drainage holes, cut away the excess roots first.

When you remove the plant from its pot, you may see that its roots have become matted. Gently loosen them with your fingers. If the mass is too dense for this, cut through the matted roots using a sharp knife. Make a shallow cut from top to bottom of the root ball, and repeat on the opposite side.

Hold the plant in the new pot to judge how much soil to put below it. Position the plant so that the top of the root ball is 1 inch from the rim of the pot. This will allow you to water thoroughly without washing away soil.

Carefully add soil around the plant, shaking the pot as you work to settle soil around roots and to eliminate air pockets. When the pot is full, press the soil gently into place with your fingers and water thoroughly.

Potting Soils

Getting the right match between plant and soil is essential. That is why there are a number of commercially packaged mixes formulated to meet the needs of different plants.

Generally, houseplants do quite well in "soil-less" potting soils available commercially. These usually are made up of peat moss, bark, sand, perlite, or vermiculite. Look for mixes labeled "premium," which may cost more but provide a well-balanced mix of ingredients. The best potting mixes are peat-based. Buy the best potting soil you can afford.

Custom mixes are available for plants with more specialized needs. Epiphytic orchids and bromeliads need a loose, organic, well-drained medium such as bark and moss. Cacti and succulents need a mix with a high percentage of sand. African violets need soil that is rich in organic matter but that drains well.

The advantages of buying premium-quality packaged mixes are that they are sterile, pH balanced, and drain well. They also maintain a light, almost fluffy, consistency that allows air to get to the roots. Avoid purchasing bagged topsoil or cheap mixes that do not list ingredients.

Your plant's well-being depends on a premium-quality potting mix that contains the right ingredients.

Propagating Houseplants

When you succeed with houseplants, you may want to try propagating your favorites.

Some houseplants practically beg to be propagated, producing *offsets* that snap off easily when you repot. Others are more challenging, which makes producing new plants from them all the more rewarding.

One word of warning: Many plant selections are patented, which makes reproducing them for sale illegal.

Stem and Leaf Cuttings

You can propagate most houseplants by rooting cuttings from the leaves or stems. First, fill rooting containers with a commercially prepared rooting medium. You may also want to buy a rooting hormone, available at garden centers, which stimulates cut tissue to produce roots more rapidly. If you use rooting hormone, do not dip the root directly into the package. Instead, put a small amount of the hormone in a separate bowl or jar. This will prevent contaminating the package and spreading disease.

Leaf cuttings. Some leaves produce new growth from the leaf tissue itself. Others form roots and shoots from the base of the *petiole*, which is the part of the leaf that connects it to the stem. African violet and gloxinia reproduce from the petiole. Rex begonia, sansevieria, holiday cactus, and most succulents reproduce from leaf tissue.

To take leaf cuttings of African violet and gloxinia, remove healthy leaves from the stem, preserving as much of the petiole as possible. Apply rooting hormone to the end of the petiole and insert it into the rooting medium so that the leaf is upright and tilted slightly backward (See **Diagram 1**). Keep the medium moist until new growth emerges and becomes large enough to repot.

The method for Rex begonia, holiday cactus, sansevieria, and most succulents involves cutting leaves into small pieces a few inches long. Dust a cut edge with

Diagram 1

Begonias are among the easiest plants to start from leaf cuttings.

Diagram 2

rooting hormone and insert it into the moist medium (See **Diagram 2**). When shoots measure about 3 or 4 inches high, remove shoots and their roots from the leaf section and pot.

Be sure to include part of the large primary leaf veins when rooting Rex begonia and other fibrous begonias, as this is where new growth will emerge.

Diagram 3

Cut triangular sections of the leaf (See **Diagram 3**). Lay these sections on the rooting medium and secure with a curved hairpin. Look for new shoots at the edge of the cuttings in about two weeks.

Stem cuttings. Most houseplants can be rooted with cuttings from stem tips. Using a sharp knife to avoid crushing the stem, cut about 3 to 6 inches off ends of healthy stems, about ¼ inch below a leaf node.

Remove half to two-thirds of the stem's lower leaves. Dip the end into rooting hormone and insert it into the rooting medium. Keep the medium moist and warm, and place it in a sunny spot but not in direct sunlight. To raise humidity, invert a jar over the cutting, or place the entire rooting container in a plastic bag. Be sure to support the plastic above the cutting's end (See **Diagram 4**). Watch the temperature carefully and do not allow it to rise above 80 degrees. Too much heat can kill the cuttings.

You can also propagate plants that have ***rhizomes***, or stems that grow at the soil surface, by cutting away a piece of the rhizome and simply laying it on top of moist soil. Propagate rabbit's foot fern this way.

Dividing Plants

Plants that grow from a central point, such as African violet, arrowhead vine, calathea, fern, orchid, and palm, can be divided by hand or with a clean, sharp knife. Carefully split the plant so that you retain thick sections of roots with each section of foliage. Repot the sections in separate containers.

Diagram 4

Start new calathea by removing leafy offsets from the base of the plant (with roots attached).

Removing Offsets and Base Shoots

A few plants, such as bromeliad, produce *offsets* or base shoots that are like miniature plants. You can separate these small plants from the parent plant to make new plants. Just be sure to get as many roots with them as possible. Other plants that produce offsets and base shoots include many succulents, Chinese evergreen, dracaena, palm, and philodendron.

Air Layering

Encourage old, large, woody plants such as dracaena and ficus to reproduce through air layering. This technique causes stems to produce new roots while they are still attached to the parent plant.

On a vigorously growing stem, choose a spot about a foot from the tip, and use a knife to injure the stem's bark (See **Diagram 5**). Scrape a portion of bark away, or cut a tiny notch through the bark.

Dust the spot with rooting hormone and wrap a thick ball of moist sphagnum moss around the site (See **Diagram 6**). Cover it with plastic wrap, completely sealing the moss, and tie in place with twist ties (See **Diagram 7**). Roots will grow from the cuts in the moss. When roots have pushed through the moss on all sides, cut off the stem just below the moss ball and pot the new plant.

Diagram 5

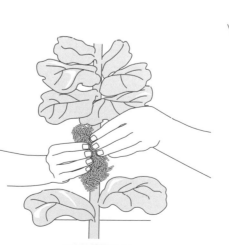

Diagram 6

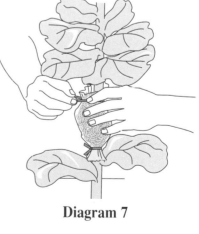

Diagram 7

Plant Profiles

The garden editors at *Southern Living* selected the featured indoor plants and flowers based on their beauty and adaptability. They range from small accent and accessory plants to large, stand-alone specimens. Most are easy to grow; some are more particular about their habitat, either because they are short-lived seasonal plants, or because their showy flowers and stunning foliage are well worth the extra attention.

Arranged alphabetically by common name, these profiles give you a description of each plant, information about its needs, and suggestions for using its color, size, and form in your home.

Many of these plants grow well within the typical indoor environment, in temperatures ranging from 65 to 75 degrees and humidity ranging from 30 to 50 percent. Plants native to the rain forest, however, may need special care. These needs are discussed, along with troubleshooting tips and solutions to help you fight the plant's pests or diseases.

When a family of plants, such as cacti and succulents or orchids, includes more than one species, the group is discussed in a single entry. The profile points out the differences in appearance and growing needs of the most popular species and hybrids within the group.

For a quick introduction to a plant, refer to the *At a Glance* box beside each profile. This will give you the major features of the plant, such as whether or not it flowers, its average size, and its light and watering requirements. The box also includes the plant's botanical name to help you avoid confusion when selecting houseplants.

Plants provide color, texture, and detail in the home. Experiment with new selections, combining and placing them to create different effects. Just as your outdoor garden changes throughout the year, your indoor garden can shift to reflect seasons and special occasions. And when you move houseplants outside to your garden for the warm months, you are also accessorizing outdoor living spaces.

A simple weeping fig becomes an elegant specimen with an underplanting of spathiphyllum, dieffenbachia, and variegated ivy planted at its base.

African Violet

African violets can be frilly like this delicate bloom.

The African violet's reputation as a fussy plant is undeserved. To satisfy its hordes of devotees, hybridizers have created thousands of easy-to-grow selections in a rainbow of colors.

Part of the plant's appeal is its compact form. The velvety green or variegated leaves grow in a crown, forming a low mound through which the flowers emerge.

As a decorative houseplant, African violet lends itself well to grouping. Placed in front of taller foliage or flowering plants, it can create a floor of color, giving an arrangement stability. Markings and flower colors can be used to add light or depth. A single plant in an attractive container makes a stunning focal point.

Pots of African violets in coordinating shades of pink and purple are grouped with maidenhair fern in a moss-lined basket.

Species and Selections

African violet hybrids range from big mounding plants to miniatures only 2 inches tall. Leaves are oval or heart-shaped, with smooth, fringed, or wavy edges. The pink, purple, rose, white, and red flowers, with shades ranging from palest blushes to deep, rich hues, can be solid or multicolored, single or double, fringed or ruffled. The newer miniatures and semi-miniatures offer this same range of options but may be only 6 inches wide.

Some African violets also grow in a rare trailing form, making them suitable for hanging baskets. Place two or three together in a small basket for a fuller look.

The Basics of Care

For best growth and flowering, the African violet needs 8 to 12 hours of bright, indirect light each day. Direct sunlight can burn the leaves. It also does well with lower levels of light for longer periods, and you can supplement with artificial lighting, if necessary.

AT A GLANCE
❖
AFRICAN VIOLET
Saintpaulia species

Features: easy-to-grow, year-round bloomer

Flowering: yes

Colors: pink, purple, rose, white, red

Height: 2 to 6 inches

Light: bright, indirect

Water: evenly moist

Pests: mealybugs, spider mites, thrips, crown rot

Remarks: vast selection of colors, markings, and sizes

African violet prefers night temperatures between 65 and 70 degrees and daytime temperatures up to 80 degrees. If a plant is placed near a window, put a thermometer beside it in different seasons to be sure temperatures stay within the target range.

While African violet will tolerate dry air, it performs better in a humid atmosphere. (See page 24 for more about increasing the humidity around a plant.)

Cold water can spot the leaves of African violet, so it is best not to water from above. Instead, set the pot in a dish containing an inch of water, or plant in a self-watering container made for violets. Always use tepid or room-temperature water, because cold water can shock the roots, and leave the plant in water only until the surface soil becomes moist. African violet should never be left in standing water. How often to water depends on the type of pot, light, and humidity, so check the surface of the soil and water when the soil has dried. Miniature and semi-miniature African violets require such small pots that they need more frequent watering. Many are now sold in self-watering containers.

If growth slows and leaf color begins to fade, feed with an all-purpose soluble houseplant fertilizer or a fertilizer specifically formulated for African violets. To avoid the buildup of salts from fertilizer, occasionally flush the soil by watering the plant thoroughly from the top, parting the leaves to avoid the foliage.

Good drainage is important for African violets. When repotting a plant, use a premium soil mix formulated for violets.

Easy to propagate. Start new African violets from leaf cuttings or by dividing a plant as it clumps and becomes overgrown.

Troubleshooting

Dark, thin leaves are a result of too little light. Pale, yellowish leaves can indicate too much light, dry air, improper watering, or need for fertilizer. Sudden wilting signals crown rot, usually caused by inconsistent watering or severe temperature fluctuations. If a plant does not flower well, it may be getting too little light or be reacting to air that is too cold or dry.

Repotting and moving a plant may interrupt flowering, but it will bloom again when roots establish in the new pot. African violet is sometimes bothered by mealybugs, spider mites, and thrips. See pages 124–125 for more about these pests.

Collections of African violets make an attractive display, such as this one on a glass-shelved étagère.

Two pots of the same selection of African violets in a terra-cotta basket are a simple tabletop accent.

Anthurium

Crystalline leaf veins and deep velvety texture are the decorative features of Anthurium clarinervium.

When you think of anthurium, you probably picture the dramatic red spathe of the flaming anthurium *(Anthurium andraeanum)*, but it is only one of more than 500 species in this large group of plants. Many are prized not for their flaming flower but for their durable, handsome foliage.

Their *spathes*—often called flowers—may not be as showy, but their foliage comes in myriad shapes and colors. Foliage anthuriums, easier to grow than their flamboyant cousins, have proven to be durable, long-lived houseplants for windowsills and other areas with medium to bright light.

Species and Selections

Anthuriums are a diverse group. Several have leaves that may reach a few feet in length, while others possess leaves that are deeply cut. You can choose from compact tabletop types and plants tall enough to be placed on the floor.

One of the most charming is *Anthurium clarinervium*. It is tolerant of a less-than-perfect environment and maintains a relatively compact size, not growing taller than 30 inches. The erect green spathes of this species add a vertical accent to the mounding plant, whose velvety leaves are dark green with silver veins.

Many foliage anthuriums are called bird's nests because their growth habit is similar to that of bird's-nest fern. They tend to be hardy plants that grow fairly large. One of the best is *Anthurium crassinervium*, which features a thick rosette of glossy, green leaves. Another type, *Anthurium crispomarginatum*, may grow several feet tall and has both narrow- and broad-leafed selections. Wavy leaf margins and a pronounced vein pattern distinguish Anthurium Fuch's Ruffle.

With its mass of broad, upright foliage, Anthurium crassinervium *is excellent for filling empty corners in a room.*

Baskets of Lady Jane anthuriums atop these room dividers provide a screen of greenery.

The best known foliage anthurium may be Lady Jane, a hybrid with glossy, dark green, heart-shaped leaves and a continuous profusion of shiny pink spathes. A more unusual member of the family is *Anthurium brownii*. Its ruffled, heart-shaped leaves are supported on long stems, and its flowers may produce a showy but inedible orange or red fruit.

The Basics of Care

Anthurium requires medium to bright light, but too much direct sun will turn foliage yellow. In a dark room, a plant will get spindly. If the light source is from one side only, turn the plant occasionally to maintain a balanced form. Anthurium prefers temperatures above 60 degrees, though some, including Lady Jane, can tolerate low temperatures and low to medium light. Daytime temperatures should be below 80 degrees.

Water thoroughly, but allow the soil to dry completely between waterings. Feed monthly with an all-purpose, soluble houseplant fertilizer. Anthurium prefers high humidity and requires it to flower, so you may not see many blooms indoors. However, foliage anthuriums are grown for their handsome leaves, not the bloom.

Pot anthurium in a premium-quality potting soil to ensure good drainage and to avoid rotting the roots and crown. To groom plants, remove mature flower stalks and any yellow leaves.

Troubleshooting

Anthuriums are relatively pest free, but they are sometimes attacked by spider mites, thrips, scales, and mealybugs. See pages 124–125 for more about these pests.

Anthurium brownii elephantasticum, with its large ruffled leaves, is a textural contrast to the trailing ivy below.

43

Arrowhead Vine

Its leaf shape gives arrowhead vine its name.

As a houseplant, arrowhead vine is valued for its distinctive leaves and clumping habit, but in its native Central America, it truly is a vine, climbing toward the treetops. What you buy is a juvenile form of the plant. As it matures, it will eventually try to stretch out of its container and change color; yet with minimal care, a young arrowhead vine can be trained to keep its color and form for years.

The common name "arrowhead vine" comes from the shape of the plant's young leaves. The 2- to 6-inch leaves range from solid green to shades of green with white, pink, or yellow markings.

Species and Selections

White Butterfly sets the standard for all other selections. The green-and-white marbled foliage is held on long, stout stems that tend to clump rather than vine and to spring back when you brush your hand across them. Eventually, it also sends out runners; cut these back to the base of the clump to keep the plant compact.

Maya Red sports a pink leaf color, especially while young. As the plant grows, the pink gives way to a rosy green color. To help maintain the distinct color patterns for at least three months, keep the plant in bright light, ideally within 3 feet of a window facing south or east. A small plant keeps its color best through the 4-inch pot size. As it matures, the plant will try to vine, so keep it cut back. This also encourages new pink leaves.

Emerald Gem offers quilted, solid green leaves that have a varnishlike luster. It also likes to clump, although not densely. To keep Emerald Gem in bounds, cut back any runaway stems. A more exotic-looking but closely related species, *Syngonium wendlandii*, is admired for the silvery white markings that flow across its deep green, velvety leaves. This one is forever trying to escape the confines of a pot, so be prepared to cut it back frequently or move it to a place where the stems can trail. You can also let arrowhead vine climb a pole made of fern bark. The vine will attach itself by clinging to the bark.

White Butterfly features white marbling on its large leaves.

AT A GLANCE
❖
ARROWHEAD VINE
Syngonium podophyllum

Features: clumps of richly variegated foliage

Flowering: no

Colors: green, white, yellow, pink

Height: 30 inches to 6 feet

Light: bright, indirect

Water: let soil surface dry between thorough waterings

Pests: aphids, mealybugs, scales, spider mites, thrips, bacterial leaf spot, root rot

Remarks: prune to control form

The Basics of Care

To encourage compact growth, give arrowhead vine plenty of light. In lower light, it will lose its compact habit, even with regular cutting back. Bright light also brings out the best color in the plant and makes the variegation more pronounced. In dim light, the green pigments in the leaf predominate, so pattern and color are muddied, but it tolerates low light well. The plant prefers temperatures between 60 and 90 degrees, but it will grow in a wide range of temperatures—from the 40s to more than 100 degrees.

Water thoroughly, and allow the soil surface to dry slightly between waterings. The dry air of heated and air-conditioned homes does not bother the plant. Fertilizer is important for the plant's health, as well as to boost color. Greens are deeper in a plant that gets enough food, providing more contrast for the bright variegation. Feed monthly with an all-purpose, soluble houseplant fertilizer in spring and summer. Be sure to *leach*, or wash, the soil every two to three months in spring and summer by running lots of water through it to keep fertilizer salts from building up and causing the leaf margins to brown. Pot plants in a premium-quality potting soil to ensure good drainage.

Easy to propagate. To start new arrowhead vines, root cuttings taken from the stems, especially those that have begun to sprout aerial roots. You can also divide a crowded clump.

Troubleshooting

Arrowhead vine has few problems, but occasionally the foliage may develop brown, water-soaked spots. When watering, wet the foliage as little as possible. If you see any spots on the leaves, remove the infected leaves at the base of the stem. Do not let your hand or the infected leaves come into contact with other leaves or the disease may spread.

Arrowhead vines can also attract mealybugs, spider mites, scales, thrips, and aphids. See pages 124–125 for more information about these pests.

Maya Red's delicate pink-splashed leaves are best appreciated where they can be seen up close.

Graphic white bands line the veins of Syngonium wendlandii's *leaves.*

The many clumps of Emerald Gem in this brass container look like a tiny forest.

Aspidistra

Upward twists of its large, leathery leaves give aspidistra unique form and coarse texture.

Aspidistra is one of the hardiest houseplants, which is how it earned another common name, cast-iron plant.

Aspidistra is a slow-growing, 2-foot-tall plant with large, leathery leaves that are held upright like blades of grass. Unlike most other plants which grow taller as their stems grow, each aspidistra leaf is borne on a single full-length stem. Thus the plant does not grow taller, only wider as it spreads and multiplies. It is one of the best houseplants for low light and is forgiving if a watering is missed.

Species and Selections

Most plants are sold simply as *Aspidistra elatior* and possess dark green leaves. A variegated form has longitudinal white markings. In the lower and coastal South, look for aspidistra in the landscape section of a nursery, as it is more commonly sold for landscaping use than as a houseplant.

The Basics of Care

Aspidistra can tolerate the low light of a windowless room but does best where it gets enough indirect light to grow a few new leaves each year. It does not take direct sun. Variegated leaves will revert to green if the plant receives too little light. Aspidistra likes cool temperatures but can tolerate hot weather without suffering. In fact, it tolerates heat well enough to serve as a deep shade ground cover in the lower and coastal South. It is also tolerant of light freezes, making it a good choice to grow outdoors on a patio most of the year.

Water aspidistra thoroughly, and allow the soil surface to dry between waterings. Average indoor humidity levels are fine; the plant can stand levels below 30 percent without the typical browning of leaf tips. In spring and summer, feed monthly with an all-purpose, soluble houseplant fertilizer. Too much fertilizer will cause variegated leaves to lose their white markings. Aspidistra does not mind being rootbound, so wait to repot every second or third year.

Easy to propagate. When aspidistra becomes crowded, divide into smaller clumps and plant in a new pot.

Troubleshooting

Aspidistras attract few insect pests but can come under attack from spider mites and scales. If the leaf tips turn brown because of dry indoor conditions, simply trim away the brown sections with sharp scissors. See pages 124–125 for more about these pests.

Azalea

Azalea, the popular landscape shrub, can also be enjoyed indoors. Florists offer a stunning array of special hybrid azaleas in full bloom. Flowers are single or double, plain or frilly, and come in the same bright colors as the landscape types. Plants that have been forced into bloom are called florist's azaleas. Use these plants singly in a pot or combined with ferns for a tabletop arrangement.

Species and Selections

You will find florist's azaleas available several times a year because they are grown in a greenhouse and tricked into bloom. Most of these azaleas are hybrids that do not withstand cold temperatures and will freeze if planted outdoors in areas where the temperature dips into the mid 20s. A few, such as Hershey's Red, Coral Bells, and Delaware Valley White, are also landscape types. In the spring, you can plant these in the garden after the last frost.

The Basics of Care

To keep a forced azalea in bloom as long as possible, give it bright light, temperatures of 60 to 65 degrees, and evenly moist soil.

Getting a plant to bloom again is a challenge. The tender florist's hybrid can go outside in its pot for spring and summer to a partially shady spot. Keep it moist, and give it monthly doses of fertilizer formulated for acid-loving plants. Leave it out until mid-fall, exposing it to several weeks of night temperatures in the lower 40s. This will initiate flower buds.

Before freezing weather arrives, bring the azalea indoors to a cool, bright window and provide a temperature between 40 and 50 degrees. This will help achieve maximum flower bud formation. Reduce feeding to once per month.

When buds have set, move to a warmer location near an east- or south-facing window, but be aware that dry indoor air can cause the buds to drop. If the temperature is above freezing, leave the pot outdoors or in the garage where the air is not dry. To control form, prune after flowering. Florist's azaleas are often rootbound and grown in a soil mix that can be hard to rewet if it becomes dry. Keep the plants moist but not waterlogged. If the soil should dry out, soak the roots in a sink full of water for a few minutes until the soil becomes wet again.

Troubleshooting

Dry leaves signal too little water and low humidity. Whiteflies and spider mites will attack azaleas. See pages 124–125 for more about these pests.

Fresh as springtime, a forced florist's azalea brings a welcome splash of color indoors.

AT A GLANCE
❖
AZALEA
Azalea hybrids

Features: dark green, pointed leaves, showy flowers

Flowering: yes

Colors: red, pink, white, salmon, bicolored

Height: 6 to 24 inches

Light: bright

Water: evenly moist

Pests: spider mites, whiteflies

Remarks: greenhouse selections must come inside before frost

Begonia

Begonias creep and crawl, cascade, clump, or rise erect. Some are grown exclusively for stunning multicolored foliage, while others produce a nearly continuous supply of pink, white, yellow, orange, or red flowers. Their often dramatic leaf forms and colors stand out when several selections are displayed together against neutral tones. Cascading plants are well suited for hanging baskets or containers that show off their graceful forms. Begonias that produce masses of flowers make good tabletop accents.

Many species of begonias are successful indoors and out. In the summer, they can dress up a porch or patio. You can even bury the pots in soil and cover the edge with mulch, and then pop them out and bring them back inside for the winter.

Species and Selections

There are so many species of begonias and they have been hybridized so extensively that neat classification is impossible. However, they can be broadly classified by the type of root: fibrous, tuberous, and rhizomatous.

Fibrous. Named for their thin, hairlike roots, *fibrous* begonias include the most popular species. They are further divided into bush types, which include wax begonias (*Begonia semperflorens-cultorum*); cane-stemmed, which include the angel-wing begonias (*Begonia* x *argenteo-guttata, Begonia coccinea, Begonia corallina* Lucerna, and *Begonia stipulacea* Acutangula); and hairy-stemmed, which include the hirsute begonia (*Begonia hirsuta*).

Wax begonias, which are also treasured as bedding plants, are succulents with thick, fleshy leaves. They flower profusely and the newer hybrids can accommodate a wide range of light levels. Wax begonias are popular in mixed arrangements in combination with ferns.

AT A GLANCE

❖

BEGONIA
Begonia species and hybrids

Features: varied forms, colorful foliage and flowers

Flowering: yes

Colors: green, white, bronze, silver, purple, or pink solid or patterned leaves; pink, white, yellow, orange, or red solid or bicolored flowers

Height: 2 inches to 4 feet

Light: low to bright

Water: let soil surface dry between thorough waterings

Pests: mealybugs, scales, spider mites, whiteflies, powdery mildew

Remarks: appreciate time outdoors in the spring and summer

Many popular indoor selections carry names from favorite children's stories, such as Cinderella, Snow White, and Curly Locks.

Angel-wing begonias are named for the shape of their leaves, which fall gracefully from bamboo-like stems. They bloom in cascades of flowers in many colors and are especially suitable for hanging baskets. Popular selections include Arthur Mallet, Christmas Candy, Cosie, and Orange Rubra.

Hairy begonias are prized for their velvety leaves. Alleryi has bearded pink flowers and dark green veins on soft green leaves. Small white flowers accent the green-and-maroon leaves of the miniature selection, Schmidtiana.

Tuberous. As the name suggests, these plants have *tuberous*, or potato-like, roots. The best known are the Rieger and elatior begonias, *Begonia* x *hiemalis*. They are prized for their colorful winter blooms and have become popular gift plants during the holidays. The single or double blossoms, in red, orange, pink, white, and yellow, sit high atop bushy green or bronze foliage. Other tuberous begonias in the group *Begonia* x *tuberhybrida* flower in summer, though they can be forced to bloom at other times of the year. These begonias include the popular rose- and camellia-flowering types and many selections for hanging baskets. These demand mild temperatures and are most popular as patio plants in the northern half of the United States and in cool areas of the West Coast.

Rhizomatous. Growing from the fleshy stems at the base of the plant called rhizomes, *rhizomatous* begonias are the largest group of begonias. These plants are admired for their unusual and often colorful foliage, though many of these begonias also produce tall stalks of delicate pink or white flowers. Best known are probably Rex hybrids (*Begonia* x *rex-cultorum*), which have asymmetrically shaped leaves. There are hundreds of Rex hybrids ranging in size from 4 to 12 inches. Popular selections include Merry Christmas, Happy New Year, and Autumn Glow.

Other popular rhizomatous begonias include the Iron Cross begonia (*Begonia masoniana*), which has a chocolate iron cross design on apple-green puckered leaves; the beefsteak begonia (*Begonia* x *erythrophylla*), a longtime favorite that has leaves shaped like lily pads with red undersides; and Jelly Roll Morton, which has light green leaves speckled with white that looks like a jelly roll.

Tuberous begonias such as this Rieger make popular wintertime gifts.

Iron Cross is a popular begonia.

Rex begonia leaves can feature a wide array of colors and often have an iridescent sheen.

The foliage of these plants is borne on long rhizomes that sometimes grow along the soil and over the edge of the pot. Leaves of the rhizomatous begonias are often textured and multicolored, and some have an iridescent sheen.

The Basics of Care

Begonias like moisture but will rot in soggy soil. Water thoroughly, letting the soil surface dry to the touch between waterings. Feed monthly during the spring and summer with an all-purpose, soluble houseplant fertilizer. Most begonias will branch if their stems are cut back. The exception are rhizomatous types such as Rex begonias whose leaves arise in a cluster similar to a caladium. Keep trailing types and cane types neat by pinching back stems that have grown too long. Pinch back to the point you want the new growth to sprout along the stem.

Fibrous. These begonias prefer bright, indirect light from a window that faces south, east, or west. They prefer typical indoor temperatures of 65 to 75 degrees during the day and cooler temperatures at night. In general, bronze-leafed wax begonias take brighter light than green-leafed selections, but they can all take bright light indoors.

Tuberous. These plants scorch in hot sun, so place them in a bright north-facing window for summer and a bright east- or west-facing window for winter. Keep the temperature between 60 and 70 degrees. In cooler climates, you can grow these outdoors in hanging baskets and planters in the summer.

Rhizomatous. Rex and other rhizomatous begonias take medium to low light, but leaf coloration may weaken in low light. Like fibrous begonias, these plants do well with average room temperatures by day and slightly cooler temperatures by night.

Easy to propagate. All begonias can be reproduced by taking cuttings from the stems and leaves. Rex begonias will grow from leaf cuttings, and rhizomatous begonias can also be reproduced by dividing a crowded plant.

Troubleshooting

Overly moist soil and extremely high humidity make any of the begonias vulnerable to disease such as powdery mildew. They can also come under attack from mealybugs, scales, whiteflies, and spider mites. See pages 124–125 for more about these pests.

Bird-of-paradise

The bird-of-paradise is a bold, large-leafed plant that commands attention. Its large, graceful leaves, often with featherlike cuts, create a sculptural effect. The name comes from the plant's flowers, which resemble boldly colored birds in flight. In summer you must move your plant outdoors to a partially shady location to bring it into bloom. But the foliage alone makes these plants worth their keep.

Massive plumes of leaves distinguish Strelitzia nicolai, *the white bird-of-paradise.*

The exotic flower of Strelitzia reginae *resembles a bird in flight.*

Species and Selections

Two species of bird-of-paradise are commonly sold as houseplants. The most common, *Strelitzia reginae*, produces a bright orange, blue, and white flower. Its oblong, pointed leaves grow in a clump 3 to 4 feet tall. The white bird-of-paradise, *Strelitzia nicolai*, has a white, pale blue, and red flower. When it is grown outdoors in tropical climates, it can rise 10 to 20 feet. Indoors, its size is more manageable, but bird-of-paradise is still a plant for showcasing against tall windows or brightly lit expanses of wall.

The Basics of Care

Bird-of-paradise plants prefer bright to indirect light indoors. If moving them outside, place the plants in shade at first and then in partial shade, where they will grow taller and flower more profusely.

Drench the plants when you water them, and drain any excess. Allow the soil surface to dry between waterings. Indoors or out, fertilize lightly during spring and summer with an all-purpose, soluble houseplant fertilizer. Their soil needs to be well drained or the roots will rot. Keep the plants looking their best by removing dead leaves and old stalks. For white bird-of-paradise, control height by removing its oldest, tallest stalks. It is normal for the leaves of white bird-of-paradise to split along the veins, giving it a charming, tattered look.

Easy to propagate. Start new plants by dividing a crowded one.

Troubleshooting

Plants grown indoors usually do not get enough light to bloom. However, you can encourage blooming by keeping it outdoors in partial shade in spring and summer. Bird-of-paradise plants are usually not troubled by pests, but watch for spider mites and mealybugs. See pages 124–125 for more about these pests.

AT A GLANCE
❖
BIRD-OF-PARADISE
Strelitzia species

Features: thick, waxy, shiny green leaves

Flowering: yes

Colors: orange, blue, and white; white, blue, and red

Height: 3 to 20 feet

Light: bright

Water: let soil surface dry between thorough waterings

Pests: mealybugs, spider mites

Remarks: good specimen plant

Bromeliad

The mottled leaves of Vriesea fenestralis *accent this sideboard.*

For those with a taste for the exotic, the bromeliad family offers tantalizing options—from small, patterned, starfish-like plants to large, arching masses of leaves with blazing red flower spikes. Bromeliads are natives of the rain forest, belonging to the same family as pineapple plants and Spanish moss. They grow beneath a thick jungle canopy in light similar to that found in the average home and are easy to grow indoors.

Bromeliads are appreciated for both their flowers and their foliage. Their flower spikes may be red, orange, yellow, pink, purple, or blue and range in size from ¼ inch to more than 15 feet long. Flowers often last for more than a month. Spikes vary in shape from the flaming swords of the *Vriesea* to the water lily blooms of the *Guzmania*. The leaves may be striped, banded, spotted, or mottled with a number of contrasting colors. Bright light brings out the depth of color.

Keep in mind that with bromeliads, too many plants of too many kinds can be just that—too much. To use more than one bromeliad, select a few plants that coordinate well and position them carefully. Try mixing plants of different heights but with similar foliage types and colors. Or use several of the same selection around the base of a larger tree-form plant, such as a ficus.

AT A GLANCE

❖

BROMELIAD
Bromeliad species

Features: exotic rosette of leaves, many with long-lasting, showy flowers

Flowering: yes

Colors: red, orange, yellow, pink, purple, blue flowers; green, gray, pink, maroon, red foliage

Height: 3 to 36 inches

Light: low to bright indirect

Water: frequent light applications

Pests: crown rot, leaf spot

Remarks: easy to grow

The bloom of Vriesea splendens *shoots upward like a flame.*

Species and Selections

Bromeliads are grouped into two broad categories: epiphytic and terrestrial. **Epiphytic** types grow above ground, clinging to tree trunks and branches and gathering necessary nutrients and water from the air and rain. **Terrestrial** types grow in the soil, obtaining moisture and food through their roots and leaves. Both types adapt to changes in growing conditions, which makes them serve well as houseplants.

Five groups of bromeliads stand out as tried-and-true houseplants: *Aechmea, Cryptanthus, Guzmania, Neoregelia,* and *Vriesea.* Each of these includes several popular species.

Aechmea. The most popular bromeliads fall within this group. Both the foliage and the flowers of these plants are colorful, and their sculptural form is lovely in just about any setting. With its dusty gray foliage and large pink-and-purple flower, silver vase plant (*Aechmea fasciata*) is one of the most popular bromeliads and is an easy and rewarding plant for beginners. Most plants in this group grow just 2 to 3 feet tall, but some, such as *Aechmea chantii* Little Harv, can fill the corner of a room. Plants in this group can be either epiphytic or terrestrial.

The large, pink bracts of Aechmea fasciata *can last for more than a month.*

This Aechmea chantii *Little Harv is actually a large floor plant.*

Star-shaped Cryptanthus bivittatus *Pink Starlight is one of the easiest bromeliads to grow.*

Cryptanthus. Plants in this group are known as "earth stars" because of the low, star-shaped arrangement of their leaves. These terrestrial plants seldom grow more than 3 inches tall and 12 inches wide. Their long, thin straplike, rippled foliage is remarkably colorful, but loses intensity in low light.

Guzmania. While some of these selections display flashy foliage, their riveting flower spikes of red, orange, and yellow steal the show. Plants in this group are mostly large, around 2 to 3 feet tall and equally wide. They are epiphytic.

Neoregelia. Generally growing 8 to 10 inches tall and 18 to 24 inches wide, these plants need bright, indirect light to produce their showiest foliage. Both epiphytic and terrestrial, they produce blue or white flowers from the center of the plant. The leaves turn red at the ***cup,*** the central water reservoir formed where the leaves join in a rosette. This gives the plants a characteristic ring of color around the flowers.

Vriesea. The upright spikes of these bromeliads often resemble red-hot pokers, but blooms also come in orange, pink, and yellow. The leaves may be solid green or mottled; the foliage of flaming sword *Vriesea* is banded. Unlike other bromeliads, these plants maintain their richest colors in low light. Plants grow 12 to 30 inches tall and wide and are primarily epiphytic. However, larger selections tend to be terrestrial.

The Basics of Care

Bromeliads do not require direct sun. In fact, hot afternoon sun can burn them. As a rule, bromeliads with thin, flexible, spineless leaves tolerate dimmer light, such as that found in the middle of a room with several windows. Those with colorful foliage or thick, fleshy leaves do best in bright, direct light or curtain-filtered sunlight.

Bromeliads require good air circulation and warm temperatures of at least 50 degrees. They also prefer high humidity and benefit from

A container filled with Neoregelia *Aztec, with its burgundy and emerald leaves, provides strong color.*

a nearby humidifier. Fertilize every two months, using an all-purpose soluble houseplant fertilizer diluted to half strength. Apply by pouring the solution into the cup in the center of the plant or by spraying the solution on the plants with a spray bottle.

Potting Epiphytes and Terrestrials

Epiphytic bromeliads do not need soil—they can grow either in bark-filled pots or on hanging *osmunda fiber mounts*. To grow epiphytic plants in pots, use a quick-draining medium, such as coarse sphagnum moss, perlite, or shredded bark, to anchor them in an upright position. With larger plants, you might need clay pots instead of plastic ones to balance their weight. To mount plants, use a piece of driftwood or a plaque of osmunda fiber. Wire the plants in place just until their roots get a firm grip; then remove the wires.

Most of these bromeliads have whorls of foliage that form a cup in the center. In the rain forest, this cup provides moisture by collecting rainwater. When watering plants facing upward in a pot (not hanging on a mount), fill this cup with tap water, brought to room temperature, about every two weeks. Let the cup become nearly empty before refilling.

To water mounted plants, spray them once or twice a week, or submerge the plant, mount and all, in water for a few minutes.

Pot terrestrial bromeliads just like other houseplants. A terrestrial bromeliad may or may not have a cup. If it has a cup, fill the cup with tap water, and water the soil about every two weeks. If it does not have a cup, keep the soil moist but not soggy. Water thoroughly and drain the excess.

Easy to propagate. Start new bromeliads by removing and planting the tiny offsets, or *pups*, that appear at the base of the plant.

Troubleshooting

While bromeliads tend to be trouble free, poor growing conditions will make them vulnerable to insects and diseases. Temperatures below 40 degrees and overwatering lead to crown rot. Injured plants may be invaded by fungi. Watch for dark spots on leaves that are sunken or water-soaked and often are surrounded by yellowing tissue. After a bromeliad blooms, the plant will produce new crowns called pups, and the mother plant will naturally yellow and die. Don't be alarmed; this is normal.

Striped foliage and large, scarlet blooms distinguish Guzmania ligulata *Tricolor.*

GETTING A BROMELIAD TO BLOOM

For all types of bromeliads, blooming depends on many variables—plant maturity, day length, light, water, and temperature—but you can induce a plant to flower. Drain all water from the plant's cup, and place both the plant and a ripe apple inside a plastic bag; tightly seal the bag for 7 to 10 days. The apple will release ethylene gas, which will prompt the plant to flower in 6 to 14 weeks.

Bulbs

Crocuses used as place markers can create a garden atmosphere.

A pot of flowering bulbs indoors in winter is like a transplanted patch of garden and a reminder of sunshine and warmth to come. Many of the hardy bulbs you buy for the landscape, such as tulips, hyacinths, grape hyacinths, crocuses, dwarf irises, and daffodils, can be forced into bloom indoors if you chill them. Others, including certain kinds of narcissus and amaryllis, can be forced without chilling.

Bulbs That Need Chilling

Producing flowers from bulbs that require chilling before they will grow and bloom indoors can be challenging but definitely worth the effort when you produce a bouquet of living flowers in winter.

Bulbs that lend themselves to forcing are often small and fragrant, so you will want to place them where you will most enjoy them: on a bedside table, beside a favorite chair, or as a centerpiece for your table.

It is best to start the bulbs in plastic pots but then transfer them into a decorative container before putting them on display. Look for unusual pottery or glassware to show off your plant's blooms.

Species and Selections

With some bulbs, every selection is a candidate for forcing. Others have a more limited list of selections that can be forced into bloom. (Refer to the chart on page 63 for some of the best selections of the following flowers.)

Forced bulbs mix well with other flowering plants, as in this arrangement of paperwhites, tulips, cyclamen, hyacinths, kalanchoes, and African violets.

AT A GLANCE
❖
CROCUS
Crocus vernus

Features: low-growing, cup-shaped flowers

Flowering: yes

Colors: blue, purple, white; solid or striped

Height: 6 to 8 inches

Light: bright to grow, medium after flowering

Water: let soil surface dry between thorough waterings

Pests: none specific

Remarks: flowers are like small bouquets

Crocus. Not all crocus species force equally well. The species *Crocus vernus,* or common crocus, is most suitable, and the selection Remembrance, with its deep blue violet flowers, is the best of these for forcing.

Daffodil. Daffodils are easier to force than tulips, but among the hundreds of hybrids, some are better than others. Do not confuse daffodils with paperwhites, which do not need chilling.

Dwarf Iris. The best species for forcing is *Iris dandfordiae,* which produces a fragrant, yellow flower with a short stem.

Grape Hyacinth. The species *Muscari armeniacum* is the easiest grape hyacinth to force. It produces highly fragrant purple and white flowers.

Hyacinth. These flowers are popular for their fragrance and because they can be forced into bloom in pots or in water. Hyacinths produce flowers that are pink, white, blue, red, or violet.

Tulip. Not all tulips that you buy for the garden are suitable for forcing. Many of the best selections for home forcing are single and double early hybrids, which tend to be smaller than the garden variety but still offer a range of colors and forms. Other good selections are found among triumph types, which are a hybrid of single early and late-flowering tulips, and single and double late hybrids.

The Basics of Care

To produce a flowering plant from these bulbs, you must put them through a chilling phase to allow their roots to develop.

How To Chill Bulbs

Hardy bulbs need weeks of cold temperatures before they will grow and bloom. (See the chart on page 62.) If bulbs have been chilled before you buy them, calculate this into total chilling time; do not let them get warmer than 60 degrees before they go back into cool conditions. The simplest way to give bulbs the cold temperature they need is to leave them outdoors if you live in an area that has night temperatures in the 30s.

Plant bulbs in general-purpose potting soil that drains well. You can put individual bulbs in pots that are slightly larger in diameter than the bulb itself, or you can set several together in a pot. For example, five tulip bulbs will effectively fill a 6-inch clay pot.

You can also do a double-layer planting. Partially fill a deep container with soil, set down a layer of bulbs, put in a shallow layer

Tête-à-tête narcissus growing beneath a ficus tree are a reminder of the daffodils that spring up under oaks outdoors.

AT A GLANCE

❖

DAFFODIL
*Narcissus species
and hybrids*

Features: attractive bright
   nodding blooms
Flowering: yes
Colors: yellow, white
Height: 4 to 18 inches
Light: bright to grow, medium
   after flowering
Water: let soil surface dry
   between thorough waterings
Pests: none specific
Remarks: easier to force than
   tulips

The scented flowers of pink hyacinths can fill a room with perfume.

of potting soil, and finish with another layer of bulbs. That way you can mix species such as tulips and daffodils. Just be sure the different selections you plant will bloom at the same time for the best effect, although a sequence of blooms is nice, too.

After planting, leave the pots in the garden where they will get the benefits of rain and sun. If squirrels or other creatures are likely to dig them up, cover with hardware cloth and weight it down.

In cool climates, you can dig a trench in a well-drained spot in the garden, place the containers in the trench, and fill around the pots with soil. Use hardware cloth if needed, and add a layer of mulch. When shoots begin to emerge, bring the containers indoors.

Where winters are too mild to cool bulbs outdoors, you can get the same results by placing them in the vegetable bin of a refrigerator. Just make sure that they are not in the same compartment with apples or other ripening fruit that produce ethylene gas, which can damage the bulb's flowers. Leave the bulbs there for approximately half of their required cooling time, and then plant them in pots.

After planting, keep bulbs between 40 to 45 degrees for the remaining cooling time so that their roots can develop as they would in the garden during fall and winter. A refrigerator or basement is an ideal location.

How To Care for Bulbs Indoors

When you see growth beginning, move the pots of bulbs to a sunny spot outdoors or a cool sunny spot inside. Keep them watered so the soil is moist and they will bloom in a few weeks.

Hyacinths and crocuses lend themselves to yet another treatment: growing in water. You can find hyacinth glasses designed for this purpose, or you can use any jar that will hold the bulb closely over the water and allow room for the bulb's roots to grow. After chilling the bulbs, place them in the glasses and keep them in a cool, dark place until roots are well developed and sprouts are a few inches tall.

Flowering bulbs will last longest if they are placed near a cool window, though it is fine to move them to warmer spots for short periods. When they are near windows, make sure that they do not touch the glass if it is freezing outside. Keep the soil moist, but do not let pots stand in water or the bulbs could rot. Turn the plant to keep it from leaning. If stems get too tall to stand upright, stake them with bamboo. Remove spent blooms to keep plants attractive.

You do not need to fertilize, since the bulbs contain all the nutrients the flowers need. Bulbs forced in water will deplete their reserves, so discard them after the flowering cycle is finished. Other bulbs can be planted outside after they bloom, but it may take a couple of years before they recover sufficiently to bloom well.

Bulbs That Do Not Need Chilling

In many homes, paperwhites and amaryllis have become almost as much of a holiday tradition as wreaths and Christmas trees. These forced bulbs are easy to grow and so rewarding that they are good plants to give as gifts.

Paperwhites are semi-hardy members of the narcissus family, and amaryllis come from tropical regions, so neither requires the complicated chilling procedure hardy bulbs need. Their long-lasting flowers make it relatively easy to time their blooms to occur when you want them. One word of caution: Paperwhites' intense fragrance can overwhelm small spaces, or even larger ones if there are several pots of the flowers. If you are scent-sensitive, use them sparingly or look for newer selections that have a milder fragrance.

Species and Selections

Amaryllis. These flowers come in many colors and variations. The blooms on standard species can be 8 to 10 inches across. Sun Dance is a fabulous big red flower; Star of Holland is red with a white star in the center. Yellow Pioneer has sunny 5-inch blooms. Miniature selections are becoming increasingly popular. Their blossoms are smaller and have longer, more trumpet-shaped blooms than the flat, flared faces of hybrid bulbs, but the stalks are apt to be just as tall. Many miniature bulbs typically produce two to three stalks, and the selection called Scarlet Baby averages three to four. Many miniature flowers are intermediate in size because of the breeding efforts made to expand their color range.

The smallest miniature selections include Salmon Pearl (coral), Charm (orange), and Spotty (freckled pink on white). Scarlet Baby (red flowers atop purple stalks) is one of the easiest to grow and is long lasting. Peppermint Parfait, Amourette, and Baby Star all exhibit the starlike pattern of the popular Apple Blossom hybrid, but they are intermediate in size and range from pale to vivid pink.

Forced red tulips are a good alternative to poinsettias or amaryllis for providing vibrant holiday color.

AT A GLANCE
❖
TULIP
Tulipa species and hybrids

Features: a wide spectrum of colors and forms
Flowering: yes
Colors: red, yellow, orange, white, pink
Height: 9 to 20 inches
Light: bright to grow, medium after flowering
Water: let soil surface dry between thorough waterings
Pests: none specific
Remarks: blooms last 7 to 10 days

Peppermint Parfait is a miniature amaryllis featuring subtle stripes on blushing petals.

AT A GLANCE
❖
AMARYLLIS
Hippeastrum hybrids

Features: wide range of colors in both large and miniature selections

Flowering: yes

Colors: red, white, pink, yellow, orange, salmon; solid and multicolored

Height: 15 to 36 inches

Light: low, medium, high

Water: evenly moist

Pests: none specific

Remarks: can bloom for many years

The miniature amaryllis Germa has an exotic appeal.

Other selections include Pamela (red and somewhat larger than Scarlet Baby), Green Goddess (white with a green throat), and Germa (white), which has long, exotic blooms.

Paperwhite. Paperwhites and other indoor narcissus that do not require chilling offer a range of colors, including white, yellow, and bicolored blooms. Flowers can range from ½ to 2 inches across and they are borne in clusters on tall stalks. Paperwhite Ziva (white) is one of the most popular selections. It produces the familiar sweet fragrance associated with paperwhites and can be forced into bloom from fall to late winter. Grand Soleil d'Or bears mildly fragrant yellow flowers and is good for forcing in late winter or spring. The selection Galilee produces white blooms with a delicate fragrance and can be forced any time from fall to spring.

Constantinopolitanus and Earlicheer produce white-and-yellow flowers with double florets. Chinese Sacred Lily features single white and yellow florets. These three pleasantly scented narcissus are suitable for forcing from late winter to spring. The selection with the weakest fragrance is Bethlehem, which produces white and yellow flowers and can be forced from midwinter to spring.

The Basics of Care

Amaryllis and paperwhites can be purchased either prepotted or as loose bulbs.

Amaryllis. To pot amaryllis bulbs, choose a container that is slightly larger than the bulb. A large bulb usually fits well in a shallow, 8-inch pot. Containers with drainage holes are preferable, but for those without them, fill the bottom inch of the container with pebbles or fine gravel and be careful not to overwater. Fill in potting soil around the bottom half of the bulb, leaving the top half exposed. Place the container next to a sunny, south-facing window—the warmer the room, the faster the bulb will grow. Some selections, such as the miniature Germa, must have heat under the pot to grow roots and bloom. Water thoroughly, but allow the soil to dry out between waterings.

Avoid getting water on top of the bulb, where it can seep into old leaf scars and cause rot. If the light comes from a single window, turn the pot slightly every few days to keep the stalk from tilting toward the light. If stalks get too floppy, stake them.

To get an amaryllis bulb to rebloom, cut off the flower stalk after the blooms have withered. Water and feed it as you would any other houseplant; then stop watering it in late summer. After the leaves have wilted and yellowed, cut them off a few inches above the neck. Store the bulb, pot and all, in a cool, dark place such as a basement or a cool closet for a month. Then check for new growth. When new leaves or buds appear, begin watering again and place the bulb in a room with moderate light and 70-degree daytime temperatures for about three weeks. In early November, relocate the pot to a sunny spot, keep watering, and soon it will reward you with a repeat performance of blooms.

Paperwhite. You can have continuous blooms by staggering the times when you plant paperwhite bulbs. Ziva is one of the earliest to bloom—it can be planted in the fall. Grand Soleil d'Or can take five to six weeks to bloom. Other selections need to be stored until late November for best results and are intermediate in bloom time. If you store paperwhite bulbs at 70 degrees, you can keep them all winter. That allows you to have flowers from fall to spring.

To keep stored bulbs from drying out, cover them with dry sphagnum moss, plastic foam "peanuts," or vermiculite. When you are ready to plant the bulbs, use a pot with drainage and one that is either attractive enough to display or sized to fit inside a basket or cachepot. Fill the pot to three-fourths of its depth with potting soil. Set the bulbs on top, shoulder to shoulder. Pour gravel up to the necks of the bulbs to hold them in place. Water well, and repeat whenever the soil feels dry. Give the roots warmth by placing the pot on top of the television or refrigerator. This should hasten root growth. Move the pot to bright light as soon as leaves and buds begin to appear. If the bulbs do not get enough light, the stems and leaves will stretch and flop over.

You can also grow paperwhites in water. Place about an inch of fine gravel or pebbles in a wide-rimmed saucer. Nestle the paperwhite down so about a third of the bulb shows above the gravel. The more bulbs you can fit into the container, the better your display will look. Fill the saucer about half full with water; then gently tip the saucer to drain any excess water.

For a unique look, anchor paperwhites in a bed of lemons.

AT A GLANCE

❖

PAPERWHITE
Narcissus tazetta

Features: intense fragrance from delicate blooms on tall stalks

Flowering: yes

Colors: white, yellow, bicolored

Height: 12 to 18 inches

Light: low, medium, high

Water: let soil surface dry between thorough waterings

Pests: none specific

Remarks: can force in soil or water

Keep the container in a cool location away from strong light for about two weeks or until roots form (a gentle tug on the bulb will let you know when roots are well developed). Then move the bulbs to a sunny window until blooms appear. Once they are in flower, move them away from direct sun. Cool temperatures mean longer-lasting flowers. Do not let the bulbs dry out or the flowers will wither and never recover.

BULB FORCING TIMETABLE

Name	Weeks of Cold	Weeks To Bloom
Crocus	15	2 to 3
Daffodil	15 to 17	2 to 3
Dwarf Iris	15	2 to 3
Hyacinth	10 to 14	2 to 3
Muscari	13 to 15	2 to 3
Tulip	14 to 20	2 to 3

These bulbs are being prepared for chilling.

GOOD CANDIDATES FOR HOME FORCING

BULB
Common Name | Color and Description

AMARYLLIS*

Common Name	Color and Description
Germa	white
Green Goddess	white with green throat
Salmon Pearl	coral
Scarlet Baby	red flowers, purple stalks
Spotty	freckled pink on white
Star of Holland	red with white center
Sun Dance	red
Yellow Pioneer	yellow

CROCUS

Common Name	Color and Description
Flower Record	violet mauve
Jeanne d'Arc	pure white with deep purple base
King of the Striped	amethyst violet, stripes
Pickwick	pale blue, striped white
Purpureus Grandiflorus	violet
Remembrance	deep blue violet with silvery gloss
Victor Hugo	violet

DAFFODIL

Common Name	Color and Description
Barrett Browning	white, small orange cup
Carlton	yellow, large yellow cup
Dutch Master	yellow, yellow trumpet
Ice Follies	white, white large cup
Little Beauty	white, yellow trumpet
Little Gem	yellow, yellow trumpet
Tête-à-Tête	yellow, yellow cup
Texas	yellow, orange double cups
Topolino	yellow, yellow trumpet
Yellow Cheerfulness	yellow, yellow double cups

HYACINTH

Common Name	Color and Description
Amsterdam	red
Anna Marie	pink
Bismarck	violet

BULB
Common Name | Color and Description

HYACINTH (*continued*)

Common Name	Color and Description
Carnegie	white
Delft Blue	lilac blue
Jan Bos	red
L'Innocence	white
Ostara	violet
Pink Pearl	pink
Viking	blue
White Pearl	white

IRIS — bright yellow

MUSCARI — white, blue

PAPERWHITE*

Common Name	Color and Description
Bethlehem	yellow
Chinese Sacred Lily	white and yellow
Constantinopolitanus	white and yellow
Earlicheer	creamy white and yellow
Galilee	white
Grand Soleil d'Or	yellow
Ziva	white

TULIP

Common Name	Color and Description
Angélique	pale pink, double late
Atilla	purple violet, triumph
Bestseller	bright orange, single early
Electra	deep red, double early
Hibernia	pure white, triumph
Inzell	ivory white, triumph
Libretto	blue-hued rose, triumph
Paul Richter	bright red, triumph
Peach Blossom	bright pink, double early
Yellow Present	creamy yellow, triumph

* do not need chilling

Cacti and Succulents

Golden barrel cactus is armed with stiff spines.

Cacti and succulents are some of the most unusual plants to grow indoors and are easy to keep provided they get plenty of bright light. The same conditions that can be challenging for other houseplants—dry air and the occasionally forgotten watering—are ideal for these tough customers from the desert.

These plants come in so many different sizes, shapes, and forms that they can serve as everything from tabletop curiosities to corner-filling architectural elements. They complement many kinds of interiors, too. The choice of containers and how the plants are arranged with other objects determine their impact. They are especially effective when several selections are grouped, which is good because success with a few cacti may turn you into a collector.

Cacti Species and Selections

The cactus family includes a vast range of plants: herbs, shrubs, vines, and trees from miniature forms to giant, towering specimens. Almost all are native to the Americas, and their unusual configurations are a result of the rugged country they inhabit. To survive, they must be adaptable, which is why so many selections make excellent houseplants.

Some of the most popular include golden barrel cactus (*Echinocactus grusonii*), old-man cactus (*Cephalocereus senilis*), and rabbit-ears or prickly pear cactus (*Opuntia microdasys*). The slow-growing golden barrel cactus is a good candidate for dish gardens.

Globe-shaped and upright growing cacti make an effective tabletop display when grouped, but must be rotated to a window to stay healthy.

Small specimens of cacti and succulents are well suited to low-maintenance dish gardens.

Even so, given the right conditions, it can grow to form a giant globe. Old-man cactus is an upright, cylindrical selection that grows up to 10 feet tall. Its long, soft spines, which resemble gray hairs, give the cactus its name. Rabbit-ears cactus, with its distinctive lobes, is a sculptural plant. It is useful in dish gardens when small and makes a good specimen plant when it reaches its mature size of 3 feet. Its spines can be irritating, so avoid touching it.

Other good selections include pincushion cactus (*Mammillaria zeilmanniana*), Peruvian apple cactus (*Cereus peruvianus monstrosus*), and bishop's cap cactus (*Astrophytum myriostigma*). Pincushion cactus is a cylindrical plant frequently sold in bloom. Its rings of daisylike flowers can be red, purple, pink, or white. Peruvian apple cactus grows upright in a twisted form, often with dramatic ridges along its spikes. Since it is a mutation, it can vary a great deal in size. Larger plants make dramatic specimens. Bishop's cap cactus is a globe-shaped plant with wedgelike segments covered with a silvery down. It grows slowly to a height of about 10 inches.

Many cacti offered for sale are **grafted** plants. They are propagated by attaching a twig from one plant to the roots of another. They include a bizarre combination of shapes and colors artificially combined to create cascading plants atop sturdy columnar bases, flowering domes held aloft, and interesting mixes of coarse and fine textures.

Cactus blooms can be large and vivid.

65

Jade plants of similar size potted in identical containers make a striking mantel display.

Succulent Species and Selections

Any plant that is thick and fleshy and capable of storing water is a succulent. The leaves and stems of succulents are like a camel's hump: They serve as a reservoir that is available when water is scarce. These plants can lose as much as 60 percent of their moisture before they begin to suffer.

Some of the most popular succulents are jade plant (*Crassula argentea*), Madagascar palm (*Pachypodium lamerei*), trailing burro's tail or donkey's tail (*Sedum Morganianum*), and hen-and-chicks (*Echeveria species*).

Jade plant is popular in dish gardens where it provides a tree-like element. It seldom grows taller than 3 feet high and features fleshy green leaves with red margins. Madagascar palm is a good specimen plant that can grow from a charming little tabletop tree to an impressive sculptural accent 4 feet tall. Trailing burro's tail is well suited to hanging baskets. Its chains of thick silvery green leaves break easily, so place it where it is least likely to be brushed against. Hen-and-chick plants are also popular for dish gardens, strawberry jars, and for succulent wreaths; they do not grow very large, but they multiply rapidly.

Other good succulents are crown of thorns (*Euphorbia milii*), aloes (*Aloe species*), and string of beads (*Senecio rowleyanus*). Crown of thorns is covered in grayish thorns. Although its leaves will drop in winter, red or yellow flowers grace the plant in spring and summer.

Each leaf of a succulent is a tiny reservoir of water.

Aloe or burn plant has stemless leaves that range from pale to deep green. Variegated selections are available. String of beads (also known as string of pearls) carries trailing stems covered with ¼-inch diameter pale green leaves. The plant is ideal for hanging baskets.

The Basics of Care

Cacti like plenty of light—they can handle the brightest sun a window facing south or west provides. Succulents also like bright light, but direct sun may burn the leaves, so place them where light is filtered by sheer curtains or does not fall on them during midday.

Most cacti and succulents grow in summer and are dormant in winter. The biggest mistake is to overwater, especially during winter when plants are dormant. However, in the summer, plants need regular watering. The best method is to thoroughly soak the soil and then allow it to dry out between waterings. Make sure the top 2 or 3 inches of soil is dry before watering. Fertilize lightly during spring and summer with an all-purpose, soluble houseplant fertilizer.

Because cacti and succulents are largely desert plants, they need a sandy potting soil that is low in organic matter. Buy potting soil specially mixed for cacti and succulents.

Most cacti have a shallow root system, and, as a result, can easily tip over in their containers, so move and handle them with care. Many succulents are just the opposite: they tend to have a stronger, deeper root system. Both are slow growers, so you only have to repot every third or fourth year. To protect yourself from painful spines, carefully wrap several sheets of newspaper around plants and secure paper with tape before repotting.

Easy to propagate. Some succulents, such as jade plant, trailing burrow's tail, and string of beads, can be reproduced by taking cuttings of the stem and leaves. Others, such as hen-and-chicks, produce offsets which can be removed and potted.

Troubleshooting

Pests are not common, but mealybugs can be a problem. See page 124 for more about this insect.

A young Madagascar palm is attractive in tabletop arrangements like this pottery grouping.

Hen-and-chicks do not grow very large but multiply rapidly in bright light and are great for filling small pots.

Caladium

Caladiums will thrive in bright light for months indoors.

The plants that brighten a shady spot in the summer garden can bring color indoors as temporary houseplants. With their many hues, patterns, and leaf shapes, caladiums vie with flowering plants for impact. Their masses of large leaves mingle well with other plants in mixed groupings, but individual plants can also stand alone.

Species and Selections

Caladiums fall into two groups: fancy leafed, which are heart shaped, and lance leafed, which are arrow shaped. Fancy leafed are the most typical and include such popular selections as the white Candidum. Many lance-leafed plants have a profusion of foliage that falls over the sides of containers, making them suitable for hanging baskets. Some of these selections include the white-and-rose White Wing, the red Rosalie, and the pink-and-white Pink Gem.

The Basics of Care

Caladiums require bright filtered light. They do well in typical indoor temperatures of 65 to 75 degrees. Water often enough to keep the soil evenly moist, but do not let plants rest in standing water. If the soil dries out, foliage will turn yellow and plants can go dormant and stop growing. Caladiums need high humidity or the leaf margins may turn brown. Fertilize lightly with an all-purpose, soluble houseplant fertilizer.

Caladiums grow from tubers sold in the spring. You can either buy plants already growing or purchase tubers and plant your own. Buying full-grown plants is not only the easiest route, you also know exactly what color the leaves are. If you decide to grow your own plants, select firm, large tubers, and plant them 1 to 1½ inches below the surface of the soil in either 4- or 6-inch pots, depending on the selection. Keep them outdoors in the shade in the spring or summer until the plants are big enough to suit you. This may take a month.

If plants send up flower stalks, cut the stalks back at soil level to encourage fuller foliage.

Troubleshooting

Long, lanky new growth can mean the plants need more light. Brown leaf margins can signal too little water and low humidity or too much fertilizer. Watch for spider mite webs on backs of leaves. See page 125 for more about this pest.

AT A GLANCE
❖
CALADIUM
Caladium x *hortulanum*

Features: large, heart- or arrow-shaped, patterned leaves

Flowering: no

Colors: green, white, pink, red

Height: 10 to 24 inches

Light: bright, filtered

Water: evenly moist

Pests: spider mites

Remarks: short-lived seasonal houseplant

Calathea

A pot of calatheas can be as colorful as a vase of flowers. With leaves in a tapestry of silver, pink, wine, purple, or green, they add sparkle to any setting. They are especially dramatic in rooms decorated in neutral shades.

Native to the jungles of South America, calatheas have made an easy transition into heated and air-conditioned homes. They are often called "second chance plants." If a plant dries out completely, you can cut it all the way back, and it will produce new growth that is tougher and even better conditioned to the indoors than before.

Species and Selections

Several selections make good tabletop plants. An iridescent, silvery green distinguishes *Calathea picturata*. It grows more loosely than most types, with a form reminiscent of a spathiphyllum. Expect it to reach 12 to 18 inches.

Colorful pinstripes on dark green, velvet-textured leaves mark *Calathea ornata*. Young plants have red stripes; middle-aged ones, pink; and older ones, white. Mature plants grow 12 to 20 inches tall and will eventually lose their striping altogether, but this takes a couple of years.

The purple undersides of *Calathea roseopicta* leaves are as attractive as the pattern on top of the large, spoon-shaped foliage. This selection grows 12 to 16 inches tall. Royal Picta is a similar but larger hybrid whose leaves are slightly scalloped. It grows to a height of 20 inches.

One of the few calatheas with solid green leaves is *Calathea gandersii* Ruffles. Yet because the leaf is ruffled and its surface iridescent, light striking at different angles gives the leaf a patterned look. You can expect Ruffles to get 12 to 16 inches tall.

Light bounces off the ripples in the leaves of Calathea gandersii *Ruffles.*

The pinstripes on Calathea ornata's *leaves look as if they were applied with a paintbrush.*

AT A GLANCE

❖

CALATHEA
Calathea species

Features: compact plants with colorful foliage

Flowering: no

Colors: silver, pink, purple, green

Height: 12 to 24 inches

Light: bright, filtered

Water: evenly moist

Pests: mealybugs, spider mites

Remarks: can revive if the top dries out

The bright centers of Calathea picturata *Argentea's leaves sparkle like its brass container.*

The Basics of Care

Be careful not to overwater and overfertilize calathea. Water it thoroughly, but let the soil get slightly dry between waterings. Drooping leaves indicate a lack of water. Calathea prefers high humidity. (See page 24 for ways to increase moisture in the air.) Feed with an all-purpose, soluble houseplant fertilizer every three months.

Calathea can survive in low to medium light, but if you want your plant to survive indefinitely, give it bright, filtered light. Watch out for full sun, as it can burn the leaves. Clean leaves with a damp cloth or put the plant in the shower, but avoid oil-based leaf shine products, which can burn calathea leaves.

Easy to propagate. To start new plants simply divide the crowded stems at their base and repot.

Troubleshooting

Do not be alarmed if the leaves fold up. This is normal behavior at night, and the leaves will unfold again in the morning. Too much fertilizer can cause leaf scorch. If you suspect fertilizer burn, leach the pot with plenty of water to reduce salt buildup. Spider mites and mealybugs sometimes infest calatheas. See pages 124–125 for more about these pests.

This row of Royal Picta, with their deep purple leaf backs, is a good example of how calatheas can fill a spot normally reserved for flowers.

Chinese Evergreen

Chinese evergreen has become one of the most popular plants for low light conditions, partly because of its durability and because it can bring a sparkle of silver, white, or yellow to an otherwise dark corner. It is a compact, bushy plant, usually growing no taller than 3 feet, which makes it effective in groupings with other plants. It can also be shown to advantage on a tabletop.

As the name suggests, Chinese evergreen is an Asiatic plant. It grows from a *rhizome* and sends up new shoots until it eventually fills its container with lush foliage. In brighter light, the leaves can stand upright, which is not as attractive as the graceful, drooping form they acquire in low light conditions.

Species and Selections

The popular Silver Queen hybrid bears distinct silver-gray markings and grows 1 to 2 feet tall. Silver King is similar, but the leaf is almost entirely silver. The basic Chinese evergreen, *Aglaonema modestum,* has an upright, arching form and dark, waxy green leaves so deeply etched with veins that they appear quilted.

A compact plant characterized by stiff, upright growth, *Aglaonema commutatum* has dark, glossy green leaves with grayish green bands. White Rajah has leaves that stand up straight and arch, and its foliage is variegated with light green stripes and creamy yellow spots on a dark green background. With leathery leaves that can grow 12 inches long and 5½ inches wide, *Aglaonema crispum* also stands out for its foliage markings. The outer margin of each leaf is dark green, but the central portion has a marbleized effect of silver gray and olive green.

The Basics of Care

Chinese evergreen likes low to medium light and does well in the soft light of a north window. Exposure to full sun can burn leaves. It prefers warm days and cooler nights but manages well in the constant temperatures produced by air-conditioning and heating. Temperatures below 60 degrees can cause leaves to yellow and drop. Avoid placing it in drafts. While this plant can forgive lapses in watering, it prefers to be kept evenly moist, but not soggy. Overwatering will quickly cause the leaves to turn yellow. Water thoroughly and allow the soil to dry slightly for best results. It also prefers moist air.

The Aglaonema Silver Queen is one of the most popular Chinese evergreens.

AT A GLANCE
❖
CHINESE EVERGREEN
Aglaonema species

Features: bushy plants with long, lance-shaped leaves

Flowering: no

Colors: green, variegations of green, silver, white

Height: 1 to 4 feet

Light: low to medium

Water: evenly moist

Pests: mealybugs

Remarks: good for low light

The compact form of Aglaonema commutatum *makes it perfect for small spaces and tabletop displays.*

Feed with an all-purpose, soluble houseplant fertilizer every month or two in spring and summer. Chinese evergreen prefers to be slightly potbound, but if it needs repotting, do this in spring.

Easy to propagate. Chinese evergreen can be reproduced by removing shoots that appear at the base of the plant. Be sure that there are a few roots attached. You can also start new plants by air layering. (See pages 36–38 for more about propagation.)

Troubleshooting

Leaf margins can turn brown if a plant is in a draft or receives too much fertilizer. If the latter is the problem, leach salts from the soil by flushing with water. Plants can develop root rot if soil is kept too moist. Mealybugs like to hide in the stems and folds of leaves. See page 124 for more about mealybugs.

Chinese evergreen's unusually patterned foliage can be used as an accent anywhere.

Chrysanthemum

Chrysanthemums are purchased for their bright familiar flowers that serve as a short-lived decoration or as a gift. If you buy chrysanthemums when the buds first begin to show color, they should last four to six weeks. Chrysanthemums sold for indoor decorations are hybrids that are different from garden mums; they are often referred to as florist's mums. If they have a shortcoming, it is that they are difficult to keep after their flowers are gone.

Mums now come in miniature versions that greatly expand their decorating potential. For simple treatment, tuck a few plants into a basket (pots and all) with one or two foliage plants and fill any gaps with moss. Use small mums in 2-inch pots to mark place settings, or mix with larger ones in an arrangement.

Species and Selections
Most florist's mums (*Chrysanthemum hybrids*) are sold by color and size. Fleurette is a newer miniature hybrid. One of the most popular Fleurette forms is the flowering tabletop tree. It has all the charm of the popular topiaries with the bonus of color.

The Basics of Care
Florist's mums can tolerate most light conditions when they are blooming, but they need about four hours of direct sun each day. They grow best in cool temperatures, 50 to 60 degrees during the day and 45 to 55 degrees at night, so place them in the coolest room in your house where they will also receive adequate light. They tolerate typical dry indoor air. Keep the soil evenly moist, but never let plants sit in water. It is not necessary to fertilize when plants are in bloom.

If you want to try to give your plants a second life after blooming, cut them back, and plant them in the garden. Because they are bred for greenhouses and not the garden, they are not guaranteed to survive winter outdoors, but many will. You will know that they are going to be perennial if they pop up the next spring. Because they are bred for a greenhouse environment, your hybrid mums may not perform as beautifully in the garden as they did when you first brought them home. However, it is worth a try.

Troubleshooting
Spider mites and aphids can attack leaves and flower buds. See pages 124–125 for more about these pests.

New miniature mums allow you to group staggered sizes of plants for more interest.

AT A GLANCE
❖
CHRYSANTHEMUM
Chrysanthemum hybrids

Features: masses of daisylike flowers in many colors and sizes

Flowering: yes

Colors: yellow, red, white, pink, orange, purple

Height: 4 to 20 inches

Light: bright, but tolerates most levels

Water: evenly moist

Pests: aphids, spider mites

Remarks: popular gift plant, difficult to rebloom indoors

Cineraria

Cineraria flowers sparkle with white rings around their centers.

Few indoor plants are treated as annuals; cineraria is one exception. It truly is an indoor annual, only one step removed from cut flowers. The bouquet of daisylike flowers blooming over its mound of large hairy foliage can be dazzling. Cineraria mixes well with other plants. You can set pots on tables, beside chairs, or before sofas, or use it on a mantel—in short, anywhere you might use fresh flower arrangements.

Species and Selections

Cineraria (*Senecio hybrids*) is a member of a vast family of plants that includes succulents and large herbaceous species. For that reason, most are commonly known by other names. Cineraria is the old botanical name for this particular group of flowering plants. The parent plant, *Senecio cruentus*, spawned masses of hybrids of varying sizes and colorations.

While many are named, plants are usually sold by flower color. Individual plants can produce hundreds of flowers, and selections come in a rainbow of colors. Many are bicolored, having a band of white circling the eye. Cineraria blooms for several weeks from late winter through spring and also offers attractive foliage. Its large, heart-shaped, furry leaves sometimes feature a reddish tinge on the undersides.

The Basics of Care

Cineraria likes lots of light but needs temperatures between 55 and 60 degrees, conditions that can be difficult to provide at home. It also prefers high humidity. (See page 24 for ways to increase humidity around plants.) Keep the soil evenly moist.

Consistent watering is important. Cineraria can develop crown or root rot from too much moisture but will quickly wilt if allowed to become dry. Since cineraria is not a permanent plant, it does not require feeding or repotting. Discard when flowering ends.

Troubleshooting

Whiteflies and aphids attack cineraria. See pages 124–125 for more about these pests.

AT A GLANCE

❖

CINERARIA
Senecio hybrids

Features: bright, daisylike flowers above heart-shaped, furry foliage

Flowering: yes

Colors: solid, bicolored; red, blue, purple, white, orange, pink

Height: 12 to 20 inches

Light: bright

Water: evenly moist

Pests: aphids, whiteflies

Remarks: discard after flowering

Citrus

itrus might not be the first plant you think of as suitable for growing indoors, but with its dark, rich foliage, sweetly perfumed white flowers, and healthy crop of fruit, it is one of the most attractive and most rewarding. Citrus trees are surprisingly easy to grow once they adjust to the interior environment. Their yield, even if small, can become the basis for delicious marmalades, baked goods, and other culinary creations.

Species and Selections

The best citrus trees to grow in containers are the smaller ones—either those grafted onto a dwarfing rootstock, which is a different species that will make trees grow smaller, or trees that are naturally small, such as calamondin (*Citrus mitis*) or Key lime (*Citrus aurantiifolia*). Most trees grown in containers will be limited in size by the container itself, but to be sure, check to see if the plant is grafted onto a dwarfing rootstock.

It is best to purchase trees that are about two years old, which is what you will usually find in nurseries. Do not be tempted to start your own seedlings; they can take seven years or more before they become mature enough to bear fruit, and even then the fruit of the hybrids will not be the same as the original fruit. If you want a tree ready to bear fruit, buy one already covered in fragrant blooms.

Calamondin (*Citrus mitis*) is a natural hybrid of kumquats and sour mandarin that grows 3 feet tall. It produces miniature fruit that is too tart to eat fresh but is delicious when used in marmalades. Kumquat (*Fortunella margarita*) produces the largest harvest of all indoor citrus trees. The selection with the sweetest fruit is Meiwa, which yields tasty small, pale orange fruit.

The two most popular lemons for indoors are Meyer (*Citrus limon* Meyer), which bears fruit like the ones you buy at the market, and Ponderosa (*Citrus limon* Ponderosa). Meyer lemon blooms and bears fruit year-round. Ponderosa only bears a few fruits at a time, but they are huge, often as big as an orange. Ponderosa's fruit has a thick rind and pithy texture, but it produces large amounts of top-quality juice. The thick rind allows it to last a long time in the refrigerator.

For limes, consider Tahiti or Persian lime (*Citrus aurantiifolia* Tahiti), which also blooms and bears fruit year-round, or Key lime (*Citrus aurantiifolia*), which has tiny leaves and small, extremely aromatic fruit. Lemon and lime trees can live up to 60 years.

A crop of lemons is the reward for a well-tended indoor citrus tree.

AT A GLANCE
❖
CITRUS
Citrus species

Features: small trees with fragrant flowers that produce yellow, orange, or green fruit

Flowering: yes

Colors: white

Height: 3 to 6 feet

Light: bright, direct sunlight

Water: let soil surface dry between thorough waterings

Pests: aphids, mealybugs, scales, spider mites, whiteflies

Remarks: some species bloom and produce fruit year-round

Calamondin fruit, ripe for the picking, makes marvelous marmalades.

Good selections of sweet oranges *(Citrus sinensis)* include Valencia and the navel orange, Washington. Mandarin oranges *(Citrus reticulata)* are also suitable for containers. Satsuma is one of the most cold hardy and is a good choice if you want a tree that will stay outside into fall. Dancy produces small but pretty, dark orange fruit. It makes a good potted plant, especially in areas where it is moved outside for the summer, as it likes the heat.

The Basics of Care

Plant citrus in a container that can be rolled outdoors in warm months and back in when the temperature drops below 50 degrees. Do not move a tree from the house into full sun, as the leaves may scorch. Put it in a spot where it will receive only early to midmorning rays. Most citrus trees need a lot of heat to produce sweet fruit, especially Satsumas and Key limes. Lemons do not need as much, making them suited to container growing in cooler climates. If you should forget and leave a tree out on a cold night, it will probably withstand temperatures near freezing, especially kumquat and Satsuma, two of the hardiest selections.

A tree that remains indoors year-round needs plenty of light to bear fruit. It will need a sunroom or a bright, south-facing window. When it blooms, you will need a pencil-sized paintbrush to spread pollen from one flower to another. Outdoors, bees pollinate the flowers to ensure that fruit will form.

When you bring the tree indoors for the winter, water it only as the soil

When in bloom, citrus's fragrance fills your home with a delightful scent.

begins to dry. If the tree drops some fruit, do not worry; it is the tree's way of reducing its load to a manageable size. Fertilize once a month in spring and summer with a fertilizer specially formulated for citrus.

Be sure to use a clay pot with a drainage hole. Start with a container at least 14 inches in diameter. Mix potting soil with sand in a ratio of 3 parts potting soil to 1 part sand. Always spread the roots of a bare root plant out like hair, smoothing them over the soil and positioning them downward. To increase the size of an established plant, repot it in a larger container. The size of the container is a check on the plant's size.

Citrus trees growing indoors in containers rarely need pruning, but if a tree becomes leggy, you can trim branches back in the spring. Since it flowers on its old wood, pruning might reduce fruit yield in the next season.

Troubleshooting

Citrus needs more magnesium than is usually present in potting soil, so use a fertilizer specially formulated for citrus that contains magnesium, iron, and other trace elements. Citrus trees are vulnerable to aphids, spider mites, scales, whiteflies, and mealybugs. See pages 124–125 for more about these pests.

A fully laden calamondin tree is a living ornament with its graceful spreading form and its wealth of colorful fruit.

Clivia

Bouquets of vivid blooms rise from the mass of clivia's straplike foliage.

You will pay more for a clivia than for most other flowering houseplants, but you will get a sturdy plant that will live for decades and bloom faithfully each year.

Species and Selections

Clivia *(Clivia miniata)* has deep coral-and-yellow blossoms that usually open in late winter or early spring. Sometimes they rise high above the plant's dark green, straplike foliage; sometimes they nestle just atop it. If the plant is in a cool room away from drafts, a single flower cluster will last about 7 to 10 days. Older clivias generally have several flower clusters that open at the same time; others follow, so the plant may remain in bloom for four to six weeks. But its striking foliage makes it an attractive houseplant even when it is not in bloom.

The Basics of Care

Clivia requires bright light, but direct sun will burn it. Place it in an east- or south-facing window where it can receive bright, filtered light. In the summer, move it outside to a shady spot. Clivia thrives in typical indoor temperatures of 65 to 76 degrees. Water thoroughly, but let the soil dry slightly between waterings and make sure the plant does not sit in water, because it is prone to crown rot. Feed clivia every four weeks with an all-purpose, soluble houseplant fertilizer.

Clivia blooms best if it has a cool dormant period to trigger the setting of buds. For about six weeks in the fall (beginning October 1 and November 1, depending on the climate), put the plant by a basement window or outdoors in the shade. During this time, withhold fertilizer and reduce watering, but do not let the soil dry out. Bring it indoors when temperatures fall below 45 degrees. In late November, resume normal watering and fertilizing.

Clivia rarely needs repotting; crowded roots often produce the best flowers. Since the plant tends to be top-heavy, weighty pots can help balance it.

Easy to propagate. Although clivia likes to be crowded, eventually a plant may get so crowded that it must be divided. Start new plants by simply dividing the parent plant into several smaller clumps.

Troubleshooting

Clivia can be injured by excess water on its crown or roots. It can also be bothered by scales or mealybugs. See pages 124–125 for more about these pests.

Crossandra

Crossandra is one of the least well-known flowering houseplants but is one of the most rewarding. Salmon to orange trumpet-shaped blooms rise from 4-inch spikes that reach outward from the plant's glossy green foliage. Flowers open first at the bottom of the spikes and bloom in a spiral toward the tips, a growth habit which has given it the common name firecracker flower.

For special occasions, display it on a table or shelves, or use it as a centerpiece if it is not too tall to block vision. To keep crossandra healthy, move it back to the sun soon afterward.

Species and Selections

In its native India, crossandra (*Crossandra infundibuliformis*) is an evergreen shrub that grows 1 to 3 feet tall. Indoors, the plant tends to stay under 2 feet tall and can be pinched to keep it controlled and full.

The Basics of Care

Crossandra needs at least four hours of direct sunlight a day to produce continuous blooms. Protect it from hot afternoon sun in the summer. It prefers daytime temperatures between 70 and 75 degrees and night-time temperatures that drop to 60 to 65 degrees. Crossandra prefers good air circulation, so make sure it is not crowded by other plants.

Keep the soil evenly moist but not wet. Make sure the pot has a drainage hole and the plant is not left in standing water. Constant high humidity promotes blooming. (See page 24 for ways to increase humidity around plants.) Feed every two weeks with an all-purpose, soluble houseplant fertilizer diluted to half strength. Remove flower stalks when the old blooms begin to die to encourage repeat blooming. Prune stems to keep plant compact and promote fullness.

Troubleshooting

Leggy growth and lack of blooms signal insufficient light. Whiteflies and mealybugs sometimes attack crossandra. See pages 124–125 for more about these pests.

Crossandra produces clusters of flared blooms that should be removed as they fade.

Crossandra's salmon blooms contrast dramatically with its deep green foliage.

AT A GLANCE
❖
CROSSANDRA
Crossandra infundibuliformis

Features: lustrous, lance-shaped leaves; trumpet-shaped flowers on spikes

Flowering: yes

Colors: salmon-orange

Height: 1 to 2 feet

Light: bright

Water: evenly moist

Pests: mealybugs, whiteflies

Remarks: flowers year-round, prefers cool rooms

Croton

Crotons are artistic accents, with their strong colors and bold markings.

AT A GLANCE

❖

CROTON
Codiaeum variegatum

Features: various leaf shapes, multicolored foliage

Flowering: no

Colors: green, bronze, yellow, red, pink, white

Height: 2 to 4 feet

Light: four to five hours of bright sunlight per day

Water: high humidity, moist soil

Pests: mealybugs, scales, spider mites

Remarks: one of the most colorful foliage houseplants

Few foliage houseplants can compete with the colorful croton for drama and variety. Though they grow tree-sized in their native South Pacific, as houseplants they are better behaved, growing only about 3 feet tall. Provide crotons with the proper conditions indoors, and you will be rewarded with a striking decorating accent. They are popular landscape shrubs in frost-free areas such as Miami and make good accents for a patio or front door.

Crotons come in several combinations of orange, yellow, red, and green and have many different leaf shapes, offering an excellent range of possibilities to complement a particular decorating scheme.

Crotons are especially effective in groupings. Older plants provide height and younger plants offer color and mass at the base, giving the same effect as a flower arrangement.

Species and Selections

Most crotons sold as houseplants are rarely named; plants with many different leaf sizes, colors, and forms will be called "croton." The croton's young leaves are green, but as the foliage matures it may become bronze, yellow, red, pink, or white. Individual croton leaves are often multicolored and may be long and narrow, curly, elliptical, or oak-leaf shaped. A variety of patterns, such as stripes and spots, occurs naturally and adds even greater sparkle to these plants. New plants should have leaves growing all the way to the base of the stem.

The Basics of Care

Croton is particular about its environment, and unless you can provide it with the proper light, humidity, and temperature, you might be better off with a more tolerant houseplant.

Place croton in a spot where it will receive four to five hours of bright sunlight a day, but keep it away from drafts. It prefers a constant, warm temperature and is healthiest when the temperature falls no lower than 60 degrees.

Croton prefers a humid atmosphere and moist soil. Water it two to three times a week in summer and every four or five days in winter, making sure the soil never dries out. Do not leave it in standing water.

Croton needs regular fertilizing every four weeks during its most vigorous growing season, spring and summer, especially if it is growing in a sunroom or moved outdoors to a deck or patio for summer. Withhold fertilizer the rest of the year.

Croton's roots do not mind being crowded in a pot, but if you need to repot, late spring is the best time. Do not feed a newly potted or repotted plant for at least two months.

Easy to propagate. Start new crotons by taking cuttings from the stem tip. Crotons like warm soil, so place your cuttings on top of the refrigerator or provide a source of heat such as a heating coil to ensure root growth.

Troubleshooting

Croton is not timid about letting you know when there is a problem. Fading leaf color indicates too little light. Dropping leaves can mean the plant needs more consistent temperatures, that the air around it is too dry, or that the plant is in a draft. Croton leaves will shrivel in air that is too hot and dry. If you overwater, the stem will rot and leaves will droop. Watch for yellow leaves and tiny webs on the undersides of leaves, which signal spider mites. Discolored leaves can alert you to scales or mealybugs. See pages 124–125 for more about these pests.

This grouping of small plants demonstrates croton's variety of leaf shapes, colors, and patterns.

Cyclamen

Cyclamen's inverted flowers are a striking contrast to its upward leaves.

Popular for gifts and holidays, cyclamen blooms when its charms are most appreciated—from fall to spring. Cyclamen's flower centers point downward while their petals rise upward. These blooms are held on long stems above variegated, heart-shaped foliage. Although flowers only last a few weeks, the handsome foliage is reason enough to keep this seasonal plant for many more weeks.

Species and Selections

Cyclamen is not sold as a named selection; selections are distinguished by flower color, foliage variations, and plant size. Cyclamen flowers range from pure white to shades of pink, red, and purple. Leaves can be deep green or marbled with lighter shading along veins. Plants may vary from 4-inch miniatures to the larger 10-inch-wide standard forms.

The Basics of Care

Cyclamen is tricky to grow, which is why it is often used as a gift and for special occasions, and then discarded after the blooms fade and the foliage begins to yellow. It prefers bright light, cool temperatures, and high humidity—three things most homes have in short supply. Flowers will last longer if the plant does not receive direct sunlight. It needs to receive four hours of bright, indirect light each day, such as near an east- or west-facing window. Cyclamen prefers daytime temperatures no warmer than 65 degrees and nighttime temperatures between 50 and 55 degrees.

Keep cyclamen moist, but do not leave it standing in water. Cyclamen also needs a humid environment. While it is flowering, feed the plant every two weeks using an all-purpose, soluble house-plant fertilizer.

Cyclamen will stop growing around April, and its foliage will yellow and wither as it enters its dormant stage, which lasts all summer. If you enjoy a challenge, you can try to bring it into bloom again. Stop feeding; store the plant in a cool, dark room; and lightly moisten the soil every two weeks. In late August, repot the tuber so that the top half sits above the soil. Then begin regular watering. New leaves will soon appear, and your plant will be ready to bloom again.

Troubleshooting

Cyclamen is susceptible to crown and root rot. Be sure it is potted in well-drained soil and follow care guidelines closely to prevent disease.

Dieffenbachia

For volume, dramatic leaf patterns, and low maintenance, dieffenbachia is an excellent choice. Dieffenbachia has eye-catching markings: spots, stripes, and solid pale centers with dark margins. Some plants look as though they are sitting in dappled golden light; others have strong herringbone markings along their surface.

Dieffenbachia is in the same family as the Chinese evergreen, but prefers more light. Several plants placed together can be a striking accent. They also combine well with other plants.

Species and Selections

An excellent low, bushing selection is Alix. Its green-and-white foliage shoots from the base, producing a fuller form than older dieffenbachias. Tropic Snow and Camille also clump, though not as fully as Alix. Tropic Snow has a creamy white pattern; Camille features creamy white leaves with green markings. Perfection has cream-and-green variegations and will grow too tall for most indoor settings unless kept in check by pruning. Rudolph Roehrs, which grows 13 to 22 inches tall, has yellow-green leaves marked with cream and a central green rib.

The Basics of Care

Dieffenbachia needs medium to bright indirect light, such as that from an east- or west-facing window. It is comfortable with typical home temperatures (between 65 and 75 degrees) and humidity. Let the soil surface become dry between thorough waterings. Feed with an all-purpose, soluble houseplant fertilizer every two to three months.

When a plant becomes crowded, you can repot it at any time of the year. Keep dieffenbachia neat by removing yellowed leaves and pruning if it becomes leggy or outgrows its space. Dieffenbachia leaves break easily, so be careful when moving.

Troubleshooting

Dieffenbachia is called dumb cane because if its sap gets in your mouth, it can cause painful temporary loss of speech. It can also irritate the skin, so use caution when pruning and keep plants away from animals and toddlers.

Dropped lower leaves can signal overwatering. If the foliage is in direct bright sunlight, you will see a bleaching or brown scalding of the leaves. Dieffenbachia can be troubled by mealybugs and spider mites. See pages 124–125 for more about these pests.

A thick mound of brightly variegated foliage distinguishes the dieffenbachia selection Alix.

AT A GLANCE

DIEFFENBACHIA
Dieffenbachia species

Features: handsome, patterned foliage; many forms and sizes
Flowering: no
Colors: variegations of green with white, cream, yellow
Height: 1 to 5 feet
Light: medium to bright indirect
Water: let soil surface dry between thorough waterings
Pests: mealybugs, spider mites
Remarks: versatile and popular for interior decorating

Dracaena

The gracefully arching leaves and compact form of Janet Craig (Dracaena deremensis) make it a great plant to place beside a chair or table.

Whatever your decorating style and space restrictions, a dracaena is bound to match the decor. Most have coarse, bold texture, with straplike leaves radiating from a central stem, imparting an exotic, tropical effect.

Many grow tall and produce daggerlike leaves, making them excellent for use as sculptural specimens. Often dracaenas are planted several stalks to a pot to give a fuller appearance and accent their sculptural form.

Species and Selections

Corn plant (*Dracaena fragrans* Massangeana) can grow 6 to 7 feet tall or more. It has 18- to 32-inch leaves that radiate gracefully from a woody stalk. The leaves are green with a gold band marking the center. The pure species with solid green leaves is available, as are other variegated selections. As corn plant grows older, it loses its lower leaves, resulting in tall stalks topped by tufts of foliage.

Madagascar dragon tree (*Dracaena marginata*) is another tall plant topped by dazzling, multicolored leaves. Tricolor and Colorama's leaves are green striped with pink and white. Like the corn plant, it can reach 6 feet in height, though it tends to be bushy when young.

Two popular selections of dracaena (*Dracaena deremensis*) are Janet Craig and Warneckii. Janet Craig is bushy and has long, narrow, dark green ribbed leaves that can measure 24 inches long and 3 inches wide. Warneckii is similar to Janet Craig but has smaller leaves marked with white stripes. These plants can grow 4 feet tall.

Sprays of slender leaves edged in pink make Madagascar dragon tree (Dracaena marginata) a distinctive specimen plant.

Pleomele (*Dracaena reflexa*) is different from the other selections in that its leathery leaves grow in a rosette. Its leaves can be solid or striped. This is another tall plant, reaching 6 feet. Its lower leaves also fall as it gets older, revealing a green cane.

A different dracaena worth noting is golddust (*Dracaena surculosa*). This plant is small with 3-inch-long leaves that are dark green speckled with creamy white. It grows in a shrublike form and rarely gets taller than 2 feet.

Ribbon plant (*Dracaena sanderiana*) is often used in dish gardens. Its leaves are green with white edges and are about 5 inches long and 1¼ inches wide. It reaches a height of 3 feet.

The Basics of Care

Dracaenas are content with low to medium light, but if you want a plant to grow taller, give it bright, indirect light. Avoid direct sunlight, which can cause leaf burn. These plants prefer temperatures between 60 and 75 degrees. They can tolerate lower temperatures, but might drop leaves if exposed to 50-degree temperatures or lower.

During warm weather, water well, keeping the soil evenly moist. Do not let plants rest in standing water. In the winter, allow the soil surface to become dry between waterings. Avoid overwatering any time of year, which can cause lower leaves to yellow and drop. New plants do not need feeding for six months. Feed established plants every three months with an all-purpose, soluble houseplant fertilizer. To prevent fertilizer salts from building up, leach the soil by flushing with plenty of water and discarding the excess.

Potbound dracaenas can be repotted any time of year. Prune tall stalks on mature plants to keep them in bounds and to stimulate new growth.

Easy to propagate. To start new dracaenas, remove the shoots that appear at the base of the plant. Or when plants become too tall, you can cut off the top, strip the lower leaves, and root it. Then provide a warm place such as the top of a refrigerator to ensure that the stem roots.

Troubleshooting

Extremely low humidity levels can cause leaf margins to brown. See page 24 for ways to increase humidity. Inspect plants for scales, mealybugs, and spider mites. See pages 124–125 for more about these pests.

*This tall specimen of the well-known corn plant (*Dracaena fragrans* Massangeana) lends itself to underplanting with small trailing or mounding plants like this golden pothos.*

Fern

Blue fern is one of the easiest ferns to cultivate indoors.

With their variety of textures and airy forms, ferns are among the most popular houseplants. They mix well with other plants in arrangements and are striking when used alone in hanging baskets, on stands and tabletops, or in pots on the floor. The trick to successfully growing ferns indoors is knowing which selections are best suited to the conditions that you can provide. You must also be willing to clean up dropped leaves in exchange for their texture and show.

Species and Selections

Ferns are some of the oldest plants on the planet, and hundreds of species exist today. Outdoors, they tend to thrive in humid, shady spots, which can make caring for them indoors challenging. In fact, many of the most popular ferns for indoors are not well adapted to the dry air found in heated and air-conditioned homes.

A good example is maidenhair fern (*Adiantum species*), which is frequently sold as a houseplant. Its delicate fronds can become scorched in dry air. The Boston fern (*Nephrolepis exaltata* Bostoniensis) also requires special care inside, though its fronds are thicker than the fronds of maidenhair. Dallas is a compact selection of Boston fern and has the advantage of less shedding. Other popular selections include Fluffy Ruffles and Florida Ruffles, both of which have closely arranged, undulating foliage; Rooseveltii, Smithii, and Verona, which have lacy fronds and a drooping habit; and Whitmanii, which also has a lacy look, but grows in an upright fashion.

In general, ferns with coarser leaves do better inside than those that have thinner leaves. Ferns that are easier to grow indoors include rabbit's foot and squirrel's foot (*Davallia species*), crisped blue fern (*Polypodium aureum* Mandaianum), bird's-nest (*Asplenium nidus*), and king and queen (*Asplenium bulbiferum*).

Dallas fern is more compact and more tolerant of dry indoor air than its fellow Boston fern.

AT A GLANCE

❖

CRISPED BLUE FERN
Polypodium aureum
Mandaianum

Features: wavy, blue-gray foliage; creeping, furry brown rhizomes

Flowering: no

Colors: blue-gray

Height: 12 to 30 inches

Light: medium to bright indirect

Water: evenly moist

Pests: mealybugs, scales, spider mites

Remarks: good specimen plant

Some hardy ferns used as landscape plants can grow well inside provided the soil does not dry out. The holly fern (*Cyrtomium falcatum*) and the Japanese painted fern (*Athyrium goeringianum* pictum) are good examples. Some brake ferns (*Pteris species*), which include several natives with colorful silver markings, make good houseplants. Give all of these bright light but not direct sun.

The staghorn fern (*Platycerium bifurcatum*) is famous for its unusual form: Its large leaves resemble antlers, and since it is an epiphyte, it grows on bark instead of in soil. Staghorn fern is often mounted on a large plaque, and in time, its leaves can reach 3 feet in length. It requires high humidity and is an excellent choice to place in a bathroom.

Sprenger asparagus fern (*Asparagus densiflorus* Sprengeri) is also a popular plant, though technically it is not a fern, since it grows from seeds instead of spores. This is a good plant to move to a sunny patio in the warm season, if you introduce it to sun gradually. Indoors it is temperamental and sheds yellow needles in low light and dry air. Fortunately, asparagus fern is quite cold hardy, and you can leave it outdoors until a freeze threatens.

The Basics of Care

Ferns prefer lower light levels than many other houseplants. Most do best with medium to bright, indirect light. They can also tolerate typical indoor temperatures of 65 to 75 degrees and do not mind dips into the 50s.

Boston and asparagus ferns can easily take temperatures as low as 40 degrees as well as very warm temperatures, which is good since the best way to care for them is to treat them as indoor-outdoor plants. They grow well outside from spring to fall; place Boston in a shady location and asparagus in partial shade to full sun. When they come inside for the winter, try to give them a cool, moist, bright spot, such as near a bathroom window. Some of the dense, needlelike foliage of asparagus fern will turn yellow and drop as the plant thins itself to adapt indoors. If you do not want to clean up the shedding leaves, move these plants to a basement or garage near a window where temperatures will remain above freezing.

Low humidity is the biggest problem gardeners face with ferns. Some, such as the Boston and staghorn, need 50 to 70 percent relative humidity to do well. You can grow these plants in a bathroom and periodically take them down and float them, mount and all, in a

Boston fern is popular for its lush, arching fronds. For best growth, keep it outside in warm weather.

AT A GLANCE
❖
BOSTON FERN
Nephrolepis exaltata
Bostoniensis

Features: long, feathery fronds

Flowering: no

Colors: green

Height: 12 to 36 inches

Light: medium to bright

Water: evenly moist

Pests: scales, spider mites

Remarks: popular, but sheds fronds easily

Holly fern is an outdoor plant that makes an easy transition to the indoors.

x

AT A GLANCE
❖
HOLLY FERN
Cyrtomium falcatum

Features: glossy, holly-like
   leaves
Flowering: no
Colors: green
Height: 18 inches
Light: medium to bright
Water: evenly moist
Pests: spider mites
Remarks: a landscape fern that
   adapts to the indoors

tub of water to keep them healthy. (See page 24 for other ways to increase humidity around plants.)

Ferns like to be kept evenly moist but not soggy. Water them thoroughly, but do not let them stand in water. An occasional rinsing in the shower will help keep them healthy. These plants are sensitive to fertilizer and must be fed lightly. In the warm months of spring, summer, and fall, feed them monthly with an all-purpose, soluble houseplant fertilizer diluted to half strength. Withhold fertilizer in the winter.

Pot ferns in well-drained soil rich in organic matter. Repot when their rhizomes become crowded. Remove fronds that become yellow or withered.

Easy to propagate. Start new ferns by dividing clumps or removing sideshoots that appear at the base of the plant.

Troubleshooting

Inspect leaves for scales, but be careful not to mistake the spores (neatly arranged on the back of the leaves) for these insects. Spider mites and mealybugs also attack ferns. These plants are sensitive to insecticides, so try removing insects by washing fronds with water, picking off insects, or removing infested leaves. If you use an insecticide, read the label carefully for information about use on ferns. See pages 124–125 for more about these pests. Shriveled leaves and brown leaf margins can indicate too little water or low humidity. Yellowed, drooping leaves can signal overwatering.

Rabbit's foot fern, with its deeply cut fronds, will grow well indoors. To show off its furry rhizomes, you can pot it in a hanging basket.

Ficus

With foliage that can be small and delicate or massive and fleshy, the ficus group offers a style of plant for any setting. Also called ornamental fig, these plants are extremely long-lived and easy to grow, and their popularity has led growers to create artful touches like braided trunks and pruned shapes.

Species and Selections

The ficus family includes more than 800 species of trees, shrubs, and vines, including the edible fig, but only a dozen or so lend themselves to the indoors.

Possibly the best known ficus is weeping or Benjamin fig (*Ficus benjamina*). Traditionally grown in tree form, it has shiny, dark green leaves that come to a fine point. Sometimes these twist slightly, giving the plant an even more graceful effect. Depending on how often you prune it and the size of its container, this plant can reach heights of over 10 feet indoors; however, most plants for sale range from 4 to 8 feet tall.

As a decorative variation, foliage growers often weave multi-trunked plants into a braid. Braided trunk plants range in size from tabletop to 5 or 6 feet tall. You can also buy variegated selections such as Golden Princess. Be sure to give these plenty of light; otherwise, they may revert to solid green. All weeping figs will have denser growth in good light.

Nuda is a ficus selection that has a more pronounced weeping form. Because the leaf nodes are close together, it has a fuller look. Although no ficus tolerates low light, this one takes lower light than most.

The pale bark of a weeping fig's braided trunk stands out against this vibrant wall color.

Ficus Alii holds onto its long, dark, narrow leaves better than many other ornamental figs.

AT A GLANCE
❖
FICUS
Ficus species

Features: trailing plants and handsome trees

Flowering: no

Colors: green, purple, variegations of green with white, yellow, gray

Height: trailing to 10 feet

Light: medium to bright

Water: let soil surface dry between thorough waterings

Pests: aphids, mealybugs, scales spider mites

Remarks: newer selections less prone to leaf drop

The rubber plant's leaves unfurl from red sheaths.

The selection *Ficus microcarpa Nitida* has a more upright appearance and slightly rounded leaves, which are less prone to drop than those on the weeping fig. It, too, will tolerate lower light. Green Gem is a combination of the best of weeping fig and Nitida. It tolerates lower light, has a mass of foliage, holds its leaves well, and is resistant to thrips. Its dense crown and closer leaf nodes make it suitable for pruning into shapes.

Rubber plant (*Ficus elastica*) is named for the sticky, milky substance secreted whenever a stem or leaf is cut. Its thick, glossy leaves grow 8 to 12 inches long and 4 to 6 inches wide. Selections of rubber plant offer a range of leaf colors from the deep purple Rubra to the yellow-green Variegata. While relatively easy to maintain, it needs to be pruned regularly by snipping off its growing tips. This will keep its height under control and cause it to produce new leaves along its stems and new shoots from the base.

One of the most interesting ficus species is fiddle-leaf fig (*Ficus lyrata*). This fast-growing plant tolerates drying out better than most, but it requires more light than the weeping fig or rubber plant. The violin-shaped leaves have a prominent yellow vein and range from medium to dark green. They grow 15 inches long and 10 inches wide. Direct sunlight can burn leaves, so place the plant where it can receive bright, indirect light.

Fiddle-leaf fig will grow to ceiling height when given enough light.

Two large ficus Alii trees anchor this settee.
They tolerate less light than most ficus.

The selection Alii (*Ficus maclellandii* Alii) has willowy, dark green leaves that grow 10 inches long and 1 or 2 inches wide. While Alii hangs onto its leaves better than most ficus plants, it will drop some leaves when it is moved to a new location. If leaf drop persists, make sure the plant receives medium to bright indirect light and is not exposed to drafts.

Creeping or climbing fig (*Ficus pumila*) has small green or green-and-white leaves that trail delicately. Not only is it unlike its cousins in growth habit, but it also prefers moist, shady conditions. Its aerial roots allow it to climb, which has led to its use as a vine to train over moss-filled wire topiary forms.

Unlike large, treelike figs, creeping fig is a small-leafed vine.

The Basics of Care

Except for creeping fig, ficus plants like plenty of bright light every day. When they do not get it, they drop leaves. When ficus plants are moved or placed in a drafty location, they can also drop leaves. This is most common with Benjamin fig, but fortunately it is quick to grow new leaves that are better adapted to the indoors.

Ficus also needs consistent watering—neither too much nor too little. Either extreme can send leaves tumbling. Check the soil often, and water when the top inch has dried out. Do not leave these plants standing in water.

Ficus plants generally will tolerate the low humidity of the indoors. Feed biweekly during spring and summer with an all-purpose, soluble houseplant fertilizer.

Ficus plants do not mind being potbound, but they should be moved to a larger container every two or three years. Use a container sturdy enough to balance the weight of larger trees.

To maintain the glossy appearance of rubber plant and fiddle-leaf fig leaves, clean them with a damp cloth or use a light leaf polish. All ficus plants will benefit from occasional hosing or showering. Prune to maintain height and form.

Easy to propagate. Start new ficus by rooting the cuttings taken from the tips of tender stems. If the stems are woody, it is best to propagate by air layering. (See pages 36–38 for more about propagation.)

Troubleshooting

Watch for aphids, mealybugs, spider mites, and scales. See pages 124–125 for more about these pests. Dropping leaves can indicate too little light, drafts, or a change in environment.

Variegated weeping fig needs plenty of light to maintain its leaf markings.

Gardenia

Gardenia's lush foliage and enchanting perfume have lured many to try growing this Southern landscape plant indoors. The plant has glossy, deep green leaves and creamy white flowers that can bloom seasonally or all year, depending on the selection. Blossoms also make excellent cut flowers.

Species and Selections

Gardenias are common landscape plants in the deep South. There are two major types: *Gardenia jasminoides*, which grows to a 3- to 4-foot shrub in a pot, and dwarf gardenia (*Gardenia jasminoides* Radicans), which has a low spreading form and grows about 1 foot tall and 2 to 3 feet wide. It has smaller leaves and blooms but is still fragrant.

The Basics of Care

Gardenia thrives on full sun, such as that provided by a sunny south-facing window. It takes typical indoor daytime temperatures of 65 to 75 degrees but likes cooler nights that are around 60 degrees. It does not like drafts. Its soil needs to be kept evenly moist but not soggy. Be sure gardenias have good drainage.

This plant requires high humidity or it may not bloom. For best results, place a small humidifier near it. Feed with a fertilizer for acid-loving plants every four weeks between April and November.

You can move gardenia outside to a partially shady spot in spring, summer, and fall until a freeze threatens. After it blooms, prune if needed to control form and size.

Troubleshooting

If indoor air is not humid enough, plants may drop leaves or flower buds. They are occasionally bothered by mealybugs, scales, and spider mites. See pages 124–125 for more about these pests.

The fragrant, beautiful gardenia bloom makes it a favorite houseplant.

Twin pots of gardenias thrive beside these large windows, where they receive both bright light and cool temperatures.

AT A GLANCE
❖
GARDENIA
Gardenia jasminoides

Features: green foliage covered with fragrant, white blooms

Flowering: yes

Colors: white

Height: 1 to 4 feet

Light: bright, full sun

Water: evenly moist

Pests: mealybugs, scales, spider mites

Remarks: difficult to grow indoors

Gloxinia

Velvety gloxinia blooms open successively, providing a spectacular show for weeks.

Gloxinia looks as if it were made of velvet. Its stunning flowers come in a spectrum of vivid hues.

It features soft bell-shaped blooms, either single or double, that are 4 to 6 inches long and up to 3 inches wide. The flowers may be crimson, carmine, pink, white, violet, or bicolored. Its foliage resembles that of its relative, the African violet. Although short-lived, gloxinia blooms over a 6- to 8-week period, with individual blossoms lasting one week or longer.

Gloxinia's rosette of foliage and showy flowers make it easy to combine with other plants in mixed arrangements. When using it alone, place the plant where the trumpet-shaped blooms are near eye level, such as on a table by a chair or a head-high bookshelf.

Gloxinia's flowers can also be bicolored.

AT A GLANCE
❖
GLOXINIA
Sinningia speciosa

Features: single or double blossoms, velvety leaves

Flowering: yes

Colors: crimson, carmine, pink, white, violet, bicolored

Height: 6 to 12 inches

Light: bright, filtered

Water: medium humidity, barely moist soil

Pests: spider mites

Remarks: stunning, large, bell-shaped flowers

Species and Selections

The gloxinias available through florists and plant shops are the result of more than a century of work by European hybridizers, although few are sold by name. Most are simply available by color of the bloom. Growers often cultivate gloxinias for selling in bloom during the holidays, but flowering plants can bloom in any season, depending on when they were started.

The Basics of Care

Handle gloxinia carefully, as its brittle leaves snap easily. Place the plant near a window where it will receive bright, filtered light but not hot sun. Allow the soil to go barely dry between thorough waterings. Use tepid water, as cold water may injure the roots and the foliage. Never wet the foliage as this could cause leaf spots. If you water from below, do not leave the plant in water more than 30 minutes.

After the final blossoms fade, the plant enters a dormant stage. At this point, you can either discard the plant or save it and try to bring it back for another season. If you choose the latter, stop watering and feeding when the leaves begin to yellow and droop. Let the foliage wither completely.

Place the pot in a cool, dry place, such as a basement, for two to three months. When the tuber is ready to sprout again, it will do so on its own. As soon as it does, resume watering and fertilize every two weeks with an all-purpose soluble houseplant fertilizer. The plant may bloom again in several weeks, but do not be surprised if it does not look as full as it first did. The size and quality of the plant's blooms and foliage will probably be inferior.

Troubleshooting

In addition to easily broken leaves and leaf spots that occur when water is left on foliage, gloxinia has few other problems. If you overwater or place the plant in too cold a spot, leaves and buds can rot. Small, pale new leaves indicate it needs feeding. If the plant gets too much sun, the leaves will harden and develop yellow splotches. Watch for spider mites. See page 125 for more about this pest.

A centerpiece of two white gloxinias is low enough to not block vision and is elegant in its simplicity.

Holiday Cactus

The fleshy blooms of holiday cactus last longest in a cool room.

If you are a gardener, make a long-lived holiday cactus part of your family's Christmas tradition. This undemanding plant will reward you with seasonal blooms year after year, and a single plant can live for decades.

Its arching stems of thick, waxy foliage yield blossoms that are tissue thin but vibrant with color. Petals are tipped with pink, salmon, red, or gold; the throat is frequently pale, showing the purple and cream flower parts to best advantage. Most plants offered for sale are a modest size, but they can grow quite large, spreading to a width of 3 feet in a generous container. They are especially striking when displayed in hanging baskets.

Species and Selections

The two selections of holiday cactus have common names based on when they bloom: Christmas cactus (*Schlumbergera bridgesii*) and Thanksgiving cactus (*Schlumbergera truncata*). Christmas cactus has flat, rounded scalloped stems; Thanksgiving cactus has teeth, or claws, along the edges of its stems. Bloom times are not exact; Thanksgiving cactus can also provide yuletide color, depending on when it was timed to bud.

The Basics of Care

In general, the holiday cactus likes medium to bright, indirect light and average or slightly cooler room temperatures when not in bloom—as low as 60 degrees is fine. Because the plant is a succulent, it can take dry air and infrequent watering; however, it will require more attention when it is in bloom.

Most of the year, the plant demands only periodic watering. You can simply set it out of the way in a sunroom or outdoors in partial sun. An advantage to moving your plant outdoors is that it will automatically set flower buds as the nights cool to 50 or 55 degrees in autumn. Bring it indoors when the tiny round buds are visible on the tip of the stems. Move the plant indoors overnight if the temperature drops below 40 degrees, and move it back out when the cold spell passes. If you keep the plant indoors where it is not exposed to cool temperatures, your plant can still set buds. Flowering also is triggered by drought and long nights that are uninterrupted by light. Be sure to give the plant bright, indirect light during the day. Keep the soil slightly dry, and place the plant in the garage or other area where lights are not turned on at night. It needs 12 hours of uninterrupted darkness at night for a period of five to six weeks or until buds form. Also give it cool nights, under 65 degrees.

Keep the plant slightly dry until buds begin forming, and then water thoroughly when the surface of the soil is dry. During blooming and growth, fertilize with an all-purpose, soluble houseplant fertilizer every 10 days.

The holiday cactus prefers a well-drained soil and likes to be slightly potbound. You do not need to repot it annually; just transfer it when the soil becomes compacted or the plant outgrows its pot. Repot when it is not setting buds or blooming.

Easy to propagate. Start new holiday cactus by rooting a terminal leaf. Simply break it off at the joint and let the wound on the cutting heal for a couple of days before inserting it into the soil.

Troubleshooting

When a white holiday cactus blooms pink the following year, it was probably kept in a low-light location or in temperatures below 60 degrees. If a plant that is ready to bloom drops buds, it probably has suffered a sudden change in humidity or temperature, which often happens when a plant is brought inside from outdoors. Try to locate it in a cool spot and maintain a good watering regimen.

The tissuelike flowers of holiday cactus can have accents of color like the pink blush on the white bloom of Snowflake.

Because their bloom time coincides with the holidays, these plants are popular tabletop decorations.

Collectors of holiday cactus are drawn to different shades of blooms, such as the nearly transparent yellow tinge of Gold Charm.

Ivy

The leathery leaves of English ivy mix well with flowers and other greenery and are also lovely on their own.

Trailing vines of ivy bring an old-fashioned accent to houseplant collections. In containers, ivy cascades over the sides, creating a graceful, flowing effect. You can mix it with other plants, planting it at the base of small ficus trees or other foliage plants with a bare trunk or placing it in containers with taller flowering and foliage plants. It is lovely in hanging baskets and can be trained into living wreaths, often called ivy baskets. It also works well outdoors on a patio and can tolerate near-freezing temperatures without browning of the leaves.

Species and Selections

Most ivies used indoors are selections of English ivy (*Hedera helix*), the same ivy that grows in the landscape. The many selections offer a wide array of leaf shapes, including bird's foot, curly leaf, fan shaped, and heart shaped. Among the dozens of choices are variegated selections and miniature forms. Needlepoint has small, dark green, three-point leaves. Caenwoodiana's dark green leaves are marked with raised white veins. Glacier has gray-green leaves with white-and-pink margins, and Gold Dust is mottled yellow and green. All selections trail typically 1 to 3 feet; plants in large pots or hanging baskets produce the longest trails.

The Basics of Care

Ivy can adapt to a wide range of light conditions; however, it prefers medium to high light. If you move a plant from one light level to another, it will need time to adjust but should adapt nicely.

Moving a plant indoors from the patio, however, can cause problems because of the drastic change from the humid outdoors to the dry, heated indoors. Leaves may turn brown along the edges, but new growth usually adapts. Pot ivy in premium-quality potting soil.

Variegated ivy provides a patterned mass of foliage as it trails over the edge of this chest.

AT A GLANCE
❖
IVY
Hedera helix

Features: trailing vine with many leaf forms

Flowering: no

Colors: green and variegations of green with silver, white, yellow, pink

Height: trailing

Light: medium to high

Water: let soil surface dry between thorough waterings

Pests: spider mites

Remarks: versatile plant, good alone and in combinations

Add some ribbon and an ornament to dress up a basket of ivy for a special occasion.

Water ivy thoroughly and allow the soil to become slightly dry between waterings. Occasionally rinse the foliage under a hose or in the tub or shower. This will discourage its nemesis, the spider mite. Feed ivy with an all-purpose, soluble fertilizer every three or four months during the fall and winter dormant season and every two to four weeks during the spring and summer.

Easy to propagate. You can grow more ivy vines by rooting the trailing stems. Pin the stems down at a node, or junction of leaf and stem, using a hairpin. After it roots, cut it away from the parent plant and dig the rooted piece. You can also reproduce ivy by taking stem cuttings and by air layering. (See pages 36–38 for more information about propagation.)

Troubleshooting
Watch for the telltale small webs of spider mites between leaves. Mealybugs and whiteflies also occasionally attack ivy. See pages 124–125 for more about these pests.

IVY BASKETS

To make an ivy basket, attach a round wire or plastic frame to a 6-inch pot of ivy. Train the plant's runners to grow along the form, clipping occasionally to produce fuller growth. When the form is completely covered, you can use the basket a number of ways:
• Place it inside a decorative container and add ornaments for Christmas.
• Weave ribbon through it and add bows.
• Tuck small flowering plants inside it, or insert cut flowers in flower picks.

Kalanchoe

Place kalanchoe amid the trailing fronds of maidenhair fern for a stunning arrangement.

Kalanchoe's compact size and long-lasting flowers are the perfect choice to provide tabletop color. Some of the newer selections offer larger foliage and long-lasting flowers in subtle shades of pink, though flowers in the old shades of neonlike red, yellow, and orange are still the standouts. After blooming, it makes an attractive, durable foliage plant.

Species and Selections

Most kalanchoes available are sold by flower color rather than by name. However, you may find named selections such as Majestic, Vulcan, and Tom Thumb. Buy kalanchoe when just a few flowers are opened. The rest will open soon and will last six weeks or more.

The Basics of Care

During winter, kalanchoe prefers bright, sunny windows and cool temperatures (65 to 70 degrees during the day, 55 to 60 degrees at night). In summer, shield it from hot, midday sun. Kalanchoe is a succulent and likes dry indoor air. Older kalanchoe selections were grown like cactus and could rot if overwatered. However, hybrids such as Majestic prefer moist soil. While they do not like soggy conditions, the blooms will last longer if the soil is not allowed to dry out. Fertilize monthly with an all-purpose, soluble houseplant fertilizer.

Kalanchoe can be difficult to rebloom, especially for the holidays. It is similar to a poinsettia in that it blooms only when days are shorter than nights. Also, the initial flowering is usually showier than subsequent ones. This occurs because the plant was grown under greenhouse conditions, which are hard to duplicate in the home.

That said, to induce reblooming for Christmas, begin on September 15 giving the plant 14 hours of uninterrupted darkness each night for six weeks. At the end of this time, buds should have formed. Place the plant in a sunny spot, and flowering should begin in four to six weeks in time for the holidays. But if you are willing to wait until spring, nature will provide the long winter nights needed to bring kalanchoe into bloom. However, plants should be in a spot where they do not receive light from a lamp that could interrupt the natural cycle.

Easy to propagate. Start new plants by taking cuttings from the stems. Let cuttings dry a few days before inserting into the soil.

Troubleshooting

Watch out for aphids. See page 124 for more about this pest.

Orchid

Many orchids, such as this Cattleya, produce intensely fragrant blooms.

Orchids have a reputation for being temperamental plants that require constant tinkering in a greenhouse to produce blooms, but many are easy to grow at home. Dozens of orchids flourish under typical home conditions; others with more particular needs can easily be induced to bloom.

Some orchids, such as the frilly Cattleya, have a fragrance to rival that of any flower. Although the foliage of most orchids is not particularly handsome or showy, the plants are so striking when in bloom that you will scarcely notice the foliage. Each bloom can last for several weeks. Because all the flowers do not open at once, many orchids will stay in bloom for two to four months. If treated well, plants will live and rebloom for many years.

Species and Selections

Orchids constitute the largest body of flowering plants on the planet, growing on every continent and at every latitude from the equator to the Arctic Circle. The plants also grow in every conceivable medium. The majority of orchids generally fall into two types: epiphytic and terrestrial. Epiphytic means that in their native environment they grow on trees or other aboveground objects. Terrestrial orchids grow in soil. This will determine how you grow an orchid at home—either in a pot of soil or in a pot of bark chips or mounted on a piece of osmunda fern bark.

Six groups of orchids include species that are well adapted and popular for growing indoors: Cattleya, Cymbidium, Dendrobium, Oncidium, Paphiopedilum, and Phalaenopsis. Another species easy to grow indoors is the Nun's orchid, *Phaius tankervilliae*.

Cattleya. This group includes the well-known corsage orchid. Of the dozens of Cattleyas, corsage orchids are intermediate in size. Those grown as houseplants offer showy flowers ranging from 2 to 11 inches across and are borne on stalks of two to six flowers each. Many are intensely fragrant. This group may be the most difficult to grow of all the orchids mentioned, but the plant is often sold in bloom, making it hard to resist. It prefers cool temperatures of 55 to 65 degrees at night and no more than 70 degrees during the day.

A BLOOM WITH NO NAME

Orchids are unusual in that they can be hybridized across species and genera, and growers have been busy doing just that for most of the 20th century. Do not be surprised if you see an orchid in a garden center that does not fall within one of the categories listed. Just ask about it, and if you are taken with its blooms and believe you can give it a good home, add it to your collection.

Cymbidium orchids come in a wide range of colors and are often used for weddings.

Cymbidium. These orchids are often used for bridal bouquets. Miniature selections are somewhat easier to grow than the larger ones, which prefer cool temperatures. The flowers of the miniature orchid are about 1 to 1½ inches wide and are borne on spikes of 2 to 40 flowers each.

Dendrobium. This group includes many different size plants, from miniatures to species that have stems 8 feet tall. They can produce sprays of 5 to 20 flowers that rise in a gentle arch as well as drooping spikes with more flowers clustered along them than you would be willing to count.

Oncidium. These plants are called dancing-lady orchids because their lips, or bottom petals, look like flaring skirts. Some are tiny; others can send out flower spikes 3 to 5 feet long. Blossoms last two to six weeks.

The pouch of the paphiopedilum gives it the common name lady-slipper orchid.

Paphiopedilum. Pouch-shaped lips have earned these plants the name lady-slipper orchid. These plants bloom in January and February, with the 2- to 6-inch-wide flowers borne either singly or in groups on spikes of varying lengths. Blossoms last one to two months.

Phalaenopsis. This is one of the most popular and easy-to-grow orchids. It is also called the moth or butterfly orchid because of the appearance of its flowers. Its succession of sturdy blossoms will last up to three months. They gradually open along a graceful, arching stalk, extending the season of bloom.

Nun's orchid. Another extremely easy and rewarding plant to grow is Nun's orchid (*Phaius tankervilliae*), named for the hooded flowers that resemble a nun's veil. Large specimens may have several 3-foot stalks, each bearing 10 to 15 white and reddish-brown flowers that last a month or longer.

Phalaenopsis flowers are usually not fragrant, but their beauty and easy care make them popular.

The Basics of Care

Here are general guidelines to caring for orchids. However, because needs can vary greatly among the hundreds of species and hybrids, be sure to also get adequate growing information from your plant supplier.

Low light is the most common cause for an orchid failing to bloom, so choose a type whose light requirements are compatible with what you can provide. Orchids for low-light settings (a north- or east-facing window) are Paphiopedilum and Phalaenopsis. Choose Cattleya, Dendrobium, or Oncidium for the bright, filtered light of an east-facing window (provided it gets three to four hours of sunlight) or a west- or south-facing window. Since direct sunlight will burn the leaves of these orchids, protect them by putting a sheer curtain at the window. Cymbidiums require as much sunlight as you can give them; a sun porch would be an ideal location.

Epiphytic orchids, whose thick stems and leaves store water, must approach dryness between waterings. The best way to water epiphytic orchids is over a sink where they can drain freely. Terrestrial types need to be constantly moist but not wet. If the soil surface is dry to the touch, it is time to water.

Most orchids prefer higher humidity than homes provide, although a few, such as Nun's orchid, do not seem to mind the dryness of air conditioning or heating. (Use one of the methods described on page 24 to provide them with moist air.) If you grow orchids in a greenhouse or greenhouse window, provide good air circulation. In all but the coolest weather, you can do this by slightly opening a window.

Nun's orchid is one of the few orchids that produce beautiful foliage in addition to stunning sprays of flowers.

GETTING ORCHIDS TO REBLOOM

If you provide your orchid with the proper growing conditions, you will enjoy years of blooms. Paying attention to a few points in particular, however, will help ensure that you get repeat blooming from your plant.

Be sure your orchid receives as much light as it requires. Many plants will survive in less than ideal settings, but they may not be able to produce flowers. Temperature is another key element in initiating flowering. If you can place your plant where the temperature drops at least 10 degrees at night, especially during the fall and winter when many types of orchids begin forming buds, you will encourage flowering.

In the autumn, or whenever your plant initiates flower buds, switch to a blossom-booster fertilizer. Be sure to occasionally flush its growing medium with plain water to rinse out accumulated salts. Humidity also affects flowering. Be sure your plant is receiving at least 50 percent humidity, especially in winter when air can be dry.

If you are growing a Phalaenopsis, you may be able to extend its blooming period. If the stalk is still green after it has dropped all of its flowers, try cutting it back to just above the first or second node. If the plant is strong enough, it will send out a branch and produce even more flowers, extending the blooming period into summer.

When Phalaenopsis orchids are placed in a basket with fern, the orchids' straplike leaves artfully mingle with mounds of delicate foliage.

You can also use a floor or ceiling fan. When the weather warms up, your orchids can go outdoors to enjoy the breezes beneath a shade tree.

Potting mixes specifically formulated for epiphytes and terrestrials are available from some garden centers and through mail order sources. Since the potting mixes naturally decompose, some orchid experts recommend repotting plants every one to two years in spring or summer to let the plants become reestablished while humidity is high.

Feed orchids once a month with an all-purpose, soluble houseplant fertilizer diluted to half the strength suggested on the label. Never feed a dry plant, because that is when the roots are especially prone to fertilizer burn.

Easy to propagate. Orchids can be reproduced by dividing the parent plant. Leave at least three shoots on each division to ensure good growth.

Troubleshooting

Scales and spider mites are the most prevalent pests of orchids. See page 124–125 for more about these pests. Avoid disease problems by sterilizing all pots and potting tools with a solution of 1 part household bleach to 10 parts water. Always isolate or discard diseased plants to prevent contaminating others.

Palm

The graceful, arching plumes of palms have kept them in favor since Victorian times, and for the best of reasons—they complement any decor and tolerate typical indoor conditions. While they are more expensive than most houseplants, their return on investment is that they are handsome specimen plants. Some selections have been known to live for decades.

Species and Selections

Palms are useful landscape plants in suitable climates, and many members of the palm family have become superb houseplants. Lady palm (*Rhapis species*), an ongoing favorite, bears clusters of fan-shaped, 6- to 10-inch-wide leaves at the ends of stalks that arch from hairy main stems. Lady palms grow from 5 to 10 feet tall and create a sculptural silhouette. But you must trim the berries if they appear, or they will leave black droppings on the floor.

Areca palm (*Chrysalidocarpus lutescens*), Kentia palm (*Howea forsterana*), and parlor palm (*Chamaedorea elegans*) are similar in that their feathery fronds arch outward in a wide canopy. Parlor palm tends to grow 3 to 6 feet tall; Areca palm will grow 6 feet; and Kentia can reach 6 to 8 feet in height. Areca is a popular palm because it is tall and

This large lady palm adds fullness and dimension to an empty corner.

The fronds of lady palm are split into seven fingerlike lobes.

AT A GLANCE
❖
PALM
Palm species

Features: lush, feathery foliage
Flowering: no
Colors: green
Height: 2 to 10 feet
Light: medium to bright, indirect
Water: let soil surface dry between thorough waterings
Pests: mealybugs, scales, spider mites
Remarks: an old-fashioned, versatile accent plant

Sago palm should be placed where its brittle fronds are not likely to be injured.

inexpensive, but it does not adapt to the indoors. Keep Areca palm on a sunny patio and bring indoors only for winter.

The Chinese fan palm (*Livistona chinensis*) has glossy fans of foliage that grow on 12- to 16-inch-long stalks. Outdoors it grows as a tree, but inside it retains a shrublike form, growing 3 or 4 feet tall.

A delicate, airy selection that grows lower to the ground is the pygmy date palm (*Phoenix roebelenii*), which seldom reaches 2 feet in height. Despite its size and appearance, pygmy date palm is a durable houseplant. For a more unusual form, consider the fishtail palm (*Caryota mitis*), whose name comes from the shape of its leaves. It eventually becomes 8 feet tall.

Another plant, Sago palm (*Cycas revoluta*), deserves mention even though it is not a member of the palm family. Its palmlike foliage sprouts above a thick, pineapple-like trunk. Take care of its leaves, which look sturdy but are easily damaged and slow to rebound. Sago leaves form a circular pattern, which is best displayed when the palm is placed on the floor where you can look down on it.

The palm's feathery form shows to advantage against deep red walls.

The Basics of Care

Palms and Sago palm do well with bright, indirect light, typical home temperatures of 65 to 75 degrees, and average to above average indoor humidity levels. Water them thoroughly, and let the soil surface become dry to the touch between waterings. Do not let the soil become soggy. Feed once a month with an all-purpose, soluble houseplant fertilizer in spring and summer.

Palms tend to grow slowly and, once mature, do not often need repotting. In their early years, repot them every year during spring or summer in soil with good drainage, but go up only one pot size at a time. A pot too large can slow growth. In summer, you can take palms outside to a shady spot protected from wind.

Easy to propagate. You can start new palms by dividing the parent plant or by removing shoots that appear at the basc of the plant.

Troubleshooting

Palms and Sago palm can fall prey to mealybugs, scales, and spider mites. See pages 124–125 for more about these pests.

Palms are good choices for open areas, such as entryways.

Philodendron

Heart-leafed philodendron is a vigorous climber. Pinching keeps it full and in bounds.

Philodendrons are great companions: They require only minimal care and survive in a wide range of conditions. They are often used in commercial settings for this reason. At home, their thick rubbery leaves withstand heating and air conditioning and the plant will last for years.

Species and Selections

While vining, heart-leafed philodendron is the well-known classic, the big-leafed, shrublike hybrids bring drama and texture indoors. Black Cardinal and Pluto grow in a rosettelike fashion, called *self-heading*, allowing them to be used as floor and tabletop plants. Black Cardinal offers intensely colored foliage; in some leaves there is not a trace of green. At first, its young trowel-shaped leaves are a bronze red. As the plant grows, the leaves get larger and rounder, and the color deepens to a purplish black. Mature leaves may be a foot long and deeply veined so that they appear quilted. With age, the color in the plant's lower leaves gradually softens to reddish green, leaving the most intense coloring on the upper half of the leaves.

Pluto is a philodendron selection that has roughly the same form as saddle-leaf philodendron (*Philodendron selloum*) but is smaller, fuller, and more tolerant of the indoors. While young, this leather-leafed plant fits nicely on a table, but as it grows, you will need to move it to the floor or a sturdy pedestal. A plant in an 8-inch pot will grow to be about 3 feet tall and 2 to 3 feet wide. Pluto does not sucker, so get a pot with several small plants. An 8-inch pot should have four stems that will grow together to form a full, mature plant.

Saddle-leaf philodendron, with its deeply cut, ruffled foliage, is used as a landscape plant in Florida. Also known as tree philodendron, this selection can become over 6 feet tall and spread at least as wide.

The old-fashioned heart-leafed philodendron, *Philodendron scandens oxycardium*, is still useful as a climbing plant that withstands low light. It can be trained along most anything—windows and doors, furniture, or pretty trellises. It will also spill over the sides of a pot and makes a good companion to plant at the base of a ficus tree.

The Basics of Care

Philodendrons do best in bright, indirect light. Black Cardinal requires soft, filtered light to maintain its color. In a room that is either too dark or too bright, its color will not be deep. Philodendrons prefer indoor temperatures of 65 to 75 degrees and are not affected by the low humidity found in most homes. Water plants thoroughly, but allow the soil to dry to the touch between waterings.

Feed plants monthly in spring and summer with an all-purpose, soluble houseplant fertilizer. Pluto should only be fertilized every six months with fertilizer diluted to half strength.

Repot plants when they become crowded. If plants produce roots above the soil, redirect them into the soil or remove them completely if they are unattractive. Cut back climbing philodendrons to control height and shape.

Easy to propagate. Start new philodendron plants by taking cuttings from the stem tips of trailing types or by removing offsets that appear at the base of clumping types.

Troubleshooting

Climbing philodendrons naturally drop their lower leaves as they grow. But if the leaves yellow and drop, the plant may be potbound; it may be in soil with poor drainage, or it may be suffering from temperatures that are too low. Aphids, mealybugs, and scales sometimes attack philodendrons. See pages 124–125 for more about these pests.

Bold, quilted leaves that range from ruddy green to deep burgundy are typical of a mature Black Cardinal philodendron.

Pluto philodendron produces shiny, leatherlike leaves and is more tolerant of indoor conditions.

109

Poinsettia

The marbling of this red and white poinsettia gives the impression of dappled light on the plant's bracts.

If any one plant is associated with Christmas, it is the poinsettia. These plants are given as gifts, stacked into poinsettia trees, and banked along stairs. When the season is over, they are usually discarded, since getting a poinsettia to rebloom takes a concerted effort. However, during their month or two indoors poinsettias are treated like a houseplant.

Species and Selections

The poinsettia (*Euphorbia pulcherrima*) grows to 6 feet in its native Mexico, but the hybrids cultivated for indoor use are kept at a neater 1 to 3 feet tall. They are compact and long lasting, often holding their color through January. Poinsettias are sold by flower color and come in a range of shades of red, pink, white, and gold. There are also selections whose color is variegated and marbled with creamy white or pink.

The "petals" of the poinsettia are actually **bracts**, or modified leaves, which surround a circle of the tiny yellow true flowers. To make sure your poinsettia is fresh, look for flowers with tight buds and with no pollen showing.

In addition to their use as potted decorations, poinsettias can be cut and used in arrangements. When cutting a stem, singe the cut using a lighted match to keep the stem's milky sap from draining. This results in longer-lasting flowers.

Look for tightly closed yellow flowers as an indication of the poinsettia's freshness.

The Basics of Care

Poinsettias like bright, sunny locations and typical indoor temperatures of 65 to 75 degrees. They prefer humid air and to be kept away from drafts, but they will tolerate a wide range of conditions as long as they are watered regularly. Keep plants looking attractive by removing yellowed foliage.

Keep the soil evenly moist, but do not let the plant sit in water. This can be a problem if it is wrapped in decorative foil. Punch a hole in the bottom of the foil and place the plant on a saucer, or remove the foil and put the plant and saucer in a decorative container. If the soil dries out or is too wet, leaves will quickly turn yellow and drop. Be sure to protect your poinsettia from exposure to cold as you carry it home from the place of purchase by wrapping it in a plastic or paper sleeve.

If you have a greenhouse and want to try to carry your poinsettia over another year, begin by pruning the colorful bracts by the first of February. After the last spring frost, plant the poinsettia and its container in a sunny garden. During the summer, cut it back to 18 inches tall two or three times, making the last cut around the middle of September. Move the plant back into the greenhouse when the nighttime temperatures drop below 55 degrees.

Poinsettias require long nights to develop new blooms. In fall (beginning no later than October 25) you must give the plant bright sun during the day and 14 hours of uninterrupted darkness at night for a period of about eight weeks. By the end of this time, new bracts will form. However, unless you have a greenhouse (with all lights turned off), providing this darkness while protecting the plant from the cold outdoors is nearly impossible. For the best color, poinsettias prefer a cool nighttime temperature of 60 to 65 degrees and a daytime temperature of 70 to 75 degrees.

Troubleshooting

Poinsettias can become infested with whiteflies. See pages 124–125 for more about these pests.

White poinsettias provide a quiet alternative to the conventional red.

Pothos

The golden-flecked leaves of pothos make it a good choice for brightening dark spots in a room.

Golden pothos, with its heart-shaped leaves and climbing form, is occasionally confused with heart-leafed philodendron, but its coloration sets it apart.

Its leaves sparkle on vines that climb up a support or cascade over the sides of a container. Golden pothos is excellent for filling out the base of tall plants that have similar lighting requirements, such as corn plants. It can also be grown in a hanging basket or trained to grow up a florist's fernbark totem.

Even in low light, pothos retains its variegated markings.

Species and Selections
The leaves of golden pothos (*Epipremnum aureum*) may be variegated yellow or white. The selection Golden Queen has leaves that are almost completely yellow. Marble Queen features marbled green-and-white leaves.

The Basics of Care
Golden pothos prefers medium light, but it can adapt to lower light levels. Unlike most variegated species, golden pothos plants will not lose markings in low light, which is one reason it is so valuable as a houseplant to brighten a dark corner. It is comfortable with typical indoor temperatures of 65 to 75 degrees, and appreciates cooler temperatures in winter when it rests. It prefers medium to high humidity. (See page 24 for ways to increase the humidity around plants.)

Water golden pothos thoroughly when the top two inches of soil is dry. Feed monthly with an all-purpose, soluble houseplant fertilizer in spring and summer. Repot when roots become crowded, going up only one pot size. Pinch back the tips of the vine every month or two to keep the plant neat and compact.

Easy to propagate. Start new pothos by taking stem cuttings and inserting into the soil.

Troubleshooting
Roots may rot if the soil is overwatered or poorly drained. Aphids and mealybugs can attack golden pothos. See pages 124–125 for more about these pests.

Primula

Primula, popularly known as primrose, is treasured for its clusters of bright-eyed, colorful flowers. Many species exist, including a large number of bedding plants and perennials, but some primulas are also used as flowering houseplants for a short time to brighten winter. These plants are usually bought already in bloom, because it takes a good deal of experience and a controlled environment, such as a greenhouse, to get them to bloom again.

Primula is a good plant for tabletops, where its cheerful flowers are shown to their best advantage. Taller species can be massed on the floor for a colorful accent. You can display primulas singly, in the same way as you would an African violet, or you can group them with other primulas and other winter flowers such as paperwhites or amaryllis. Their coarse leaf texture also contrasts nicely with the finer-leafed asparagus or maidenhair ferns.

Species and Selections

The species *Primula malacoides*, or fairy primrose, is the largest of the indoor primulas, growing as tall as 18 inches. Its scented clumps of single or double blossoms rise above ruffled green foliage.

Florist's primrose (*Primula sinensis*) comes in a wide array of colors and grows to 12 inches tall. Called the poison primrose because it can irritate sensitive skin, *Primula obconica* produces flowers throughout the year and grows to 10 inches. The flowers of *Primula acaulis* have no stalks. They nestle in the center of the plant surrounded by a rosette of foliage.

The Basics of Care

Primula prefers bright, indirect light and cool temperatures (45 to 50 degrees at night, 55 to 60 degrees during the daytime). It likes humid air and evenly moist soil. Water thoroughly, but do not let the plant sit in water. It does not need fertilizer when it is in bloom. You may have a difficult time keeping primula, which is a cool-weather plant, alive through summer. It is also difficult to bring back into bloom without a greenhouse. Most people simply enjoy their primula for a few weeks in winter and then compost it.

Troubleshooting

Primula can be troubled by spider mites. See pages 124–125 for more about spider mites. Drafts and dry air can scorch leaves.

Primulas look especially festive when several colors and sizes are grouped.

AT A GLANCE
❖
PRIMULA
Primula species

Features: clustered tiers of bright, seasonal flowers

Flowering: yes

Colors: red, pink, yellow, white, blue

Height: 12 to 18 inches

Light: medium to bright, indirect

Water: evenly moist

Pests: spider mites

Remarks: seasonal tabletop plant

Sansevieria

The strong vertical form of Bantel's Sensation delivers height without too much width.

If you are looking for a plant to give to a brown thumb, sansevieria is a good choice. The quickest way to harm this plant is to give it too much attention. Sansevieria is a succulent, and its thick, leathery leaves take care of its needs.

These plants range widely in size and form, making them useful for everything from dish gardens to tabletops. The bladelike leaves of the taller varieties provide an artistic silhouette from a distance. All of these plants are shown to best advantage in interesting containers. They group well and can provide light and pattern to dark spaces in a room.

Species and Selections

The most common houseplant of the group is *Sansevieria trifasciata*, which goes by the unflattering names of snake plant or mother-in-law's tongue. Its familiar form is a clump of erect, straplike leaves that reach about 3 feet tall and are marked with irregular gray or light green crossbands characteristic of many sansevierias. The selection *Sansevieria trifasciata* Laurentii has an identical form, but its leaves are dressed with a margin of gold. Bantel's Sensation has markings quite similar to snake plant but adds white stripes that run the length of its tall, slender leaves. The extent of the white marking varies from leaf to leaf.

Sansevierias offer a range of shorter selections as well. Futura has markings similar to Laurentii's, but the leaves are wider and grow no higher than 15 inches. Robusta is similar to Futura but without the golden leaf margins. An even smaller version is bird's-nest sansevieria, a 3- to 4-inch tall rosette. It forms a 6-inch-wide clump of deep green leaves with crossbands like those of snake plant. Because it suckers from the base, a single plant

Compact, wide-leafed Futura is just the right size for a centerpiece.

fills a pot with a mosaic of rosettes. Golden Hahnii is a similar selection but features leaves banded in creamy gold. Silver Hahnii has deep green crossbands on silvery green leaves.

Spear sansevieria (*Sansevieria cylindrica*) stands out from the rest because of its foliage, which curls into a stiff spearlike form that hardly looks like a leaf. Arching under their own weight, the 2- to 3-foot-long leaves form a broad ray shape.

Golden Hahnii has lighter tones and a more graceful form than more typical sansevierias.

The Basics of Care

The best way to care for sansevierias is to slightly ignore them. They can take a wide range of light conditions and are comfortable with typical indoor temperatures of 65 to 75 degrees and dry indoor air. Sansevierias grown in bright light can add as many as a dozen new leaves each year. They may need twice as much water and fertilizer, though, as plants grown in low light. Water only when the soil feels dry about two inches below the surface. Do not pour water directly into the clump, as this invites rotting. Feed growing plants every two months with an all-purpose, soluble houseplant fertilizer; plants in lower light can be fed every six months.

Because many of these plants grow as high as 3 feet, they need heavy 8-inch pots to provide counterweight. Sansevierias do not mind being potbound. Repot every two years or whenever the roots start growing out of the pot's drainage holes.

Easy to propagate. To start new sansevieria plants, separate a plant into several smaller clumps and repot them.

Troubleshooting

Plants left sitting in water can develop root rot.

The spearlike leaves of Sansevieria cylindrica *create a living sculpture.*

Schefflera

This braided-trunk dwarf schefflera was clipped into a topiary form to make it a lovely tabletop plant.

Schefflera is an Australian import that has become an all-American houseplant. The umbrella tree, with its large, whorled leaves, was the first schefflera to become popular. Dwarf types have also come along, and now there is a selection for just about any spot a tree is needed.

Species and Selections

The umbrella tree (*Brassaia actinophylla*) can grow 40 feet tall in its native habitat. In the home, it tends to stop between 8 and 10 feet, but it tolerates heavy pruning if it gets out of bounds. Its large, 18-inch-long leaves look as though they could provide shelter in a downpour.

Dwarf schefflera (*Schefflera arboricola*) can grow as tall as umbrella tree, but its leaves are less than half as big and the plant grows more slowly. It is more compact, with less space between the whorls of foliage. Renate is a European selection of dwarf schefflera that features a finer texture and a more compact canopy than the regular dwarf. It has smooth, shiny, deep green leaves that are slightly lobed to give the plant a soft, lacy look. A slow grower, Renate will stay neat and compact if you place it in bright light. Without enough light, the leaves will start dropping. Variegata, a selection with creamy markings on the leaves, also needs bright light to retain its brilliance.

The Basics of Care

Scheffleras do well in direct sunlight or bright, indirect light. They tolerate typical indoor temperatures of 65 to 75 degrees and average humidity levels. Water thoroughly, and let the soil go slightly dry between times. Feed every three months (or, in the case of Renate, every six months) with an all-purpose, soluble houseplant fertilizer. Excellent drainage is a must. When plants get severely rootbound, repot any time of the year. Prune plants to control height; encourage

AT A GLANCE
❖
DWARF SCHEFFLERA
Schefflera arboricola

Features: whorls of foliage on bushing or treelike specimen plants

Flowering: no

Colors: green, variegated

Height: 3 to 10 feet

Light: full sun to bright indirect

Water: let soil surface dry between thorough waterings

Pests: aphids, spider mites

Remarks: can prune to control shape and height

branching by making a cut in the place where you want new growth to sprout. Keep plants neat by removing yellowed foliage.

Easy to propagate. Start new schefflera plants by rooting cuttings from the stem tips. Be sure to keep the cuttings warm and moist until they root.

Troubleshooting

Scheffleras can fall prey to aphids and spider mites. The large-leafed umbrella tree is particularly susceptible to spider mites and for that reason is less popular than dwarf schefflera. See pages 124–125 for more about these pests.

For a striking table-top decoration, a variegated dwarf schefflera is embellished with a temporary arrangement of Boston ferns, pothos, fragrant rubrum lilies, and floribunda roses.

Spathiphyllum

This spathiphyllum is complemented by a base of coral impatiens and trailing ivy.

Spathiphyllum, also known as spathe flower and peace lily, is an undemanding plant. The spathes, or white bracts cupped around the plant's flower stalk, give away the fact that spathiphyllum and anthurium are related. But unlike its showy cousin, spathiphyllum's cool green-and-white coloration seems more suited to a veranda than to center stage. Spathiphyllum should be where its foliage provides interesting contrast and its fragrant flowers can be appreciated, for example near chairs and sofas, in entryways, and beside windows that let in a gentle breeze.

Species and Selections

Spathiphyllum selections vary primarily in their size and leaf characteristics. Some plants have deeply quilted leaves; others have thinner, more graceful foliage. Color can range from a bright medium green to a deep, almost black green, and leaves can be glossy or matte.

Spathiphyllum wallisii is a compact plant that grows 12 inches tall. It produces 4-inch-long flowers for weeks at a time. Hybrid selections include Mauna Loa, which typically grows to 3 feet tall, though it can reach heights of 6 feet in large enough pots. Its flower stalks can become 20 inches long and its flowers can be 8 inches long. With its waxy green leaves, Mauna Loa is an attractive plant even when not in bloom and is one of the most commonly found selections.

Clevelandii is an early hybrid that is slightly smaller in scale than *wallisii*. It has been replaced in many garden centers by selections that grow faster. The smallest selection is Petite, which stays between 12 and 20 inches and produces a profusion of small blooms.

At the other end of the spectrum is Sensation, a hybrid that can grow to more than 5 feet tall. It features white flowers as large as 8 inches and large, deep green, leathery leaves that make the plant more drought tolerant than thinner-leafed selections. DeNeve is a fast-growing selection that reaches 2½ feet and features light green matte leaves that are serrated. Tasson grows 1½ to 2 feet and has deep, glossy leaves with wavy edges. Viscount Prima is similar to Tasson but grows to 2 feet and has wider, darker leaves.

The Basics of Care

Spathiphyllum tolerates low light, but it needs 4 to 6 hours of bright, indirect light each day to bloom. It is comfortable at home temperatures of 65 to 75 degrees and the dry air typical of indoors.

For best results, keep the plant's soil evenly moist, but do not let the plant stand in water. Feed monthly in spring and summer with an all-purpose, soluble houseplant fertilizer. Repot each spring. Remove yellow leaves and spent flower stalks to keep the plant neat.

Controlling Size

Overall size of spathiphyllum can be controlled by the size of the plant's pot. For example, a Sensation grown in a 10-inch pot will typically reach 3 feet high. Because spathiphyllums spread by rhizomes, they can be divided and repotted if they threaten to outgrow their location. These plants typically bloom in spring and summer, and in optimum conditions, they can flower more frequently. Their flowers have a candylike fragrance and produce a relatively large amount of pollen, which can leave a white dusting on the leaves and can sometimes irritate sensitive noses.

Easy to propagate. To start new spathiphyllum plants, divide a crowded plant into several smaller clumps and repot.

Troubleshooting

Lack of flowering indicates light levels are too low. Inadequate drainage can cause root rot. Aphids, mealybugs, and spider mites can attack spathiphyllums. See pages 124–125 for more about these pests. Leaves may develop brown tips, especially if the plants become dry between waterings. Keep the soil moist, and trim away the brown tips.

The upright form of spathiphyllum is light and airy and lends itself to underplanting with fine-leafed companion plants.

A breeze through the window will carry spathiphyllum's scent throughout the room.

119

Streptocarpus

Trumpet-shaped blossoms of streptocarpus ride atop long, thin stems.

If you have had success growing African violets, you need to try another member of the same family, streptocarpus. Many of its needs are the same, and its vivid trumpet-shaped blossoms are as alluring as those of the African violet, only larger.

You can display plants in decorative containers on end tables or coffee tables or use them as centerpieces for dining room or kitchen tables. They are also excellent for growing in hanging baskets and dish gardens. Streptocarpus also make a nice addition to an indoor arrangement that combines ferns and colorful seasonal plants.

Species and Selections

Also known as cape primrose, the showiest streptocarpus selections are large-flowered hybrids. Unlike older selections which had large leaves and fewer flowers, the newer hybrids are more compact with smaller leaves and many more flowers. Growing 8 to 12 inches tall, the cape primrose features long, quilted, hairy leaves that resemble those of the *Primula* species. Flowering is spectacular throughout the year. Borne atop long, thin stems, the trumpet-shaped blossoms may be blue, violet, red, pink, or white. Many are bicolored. Like an African violet, streptocarpus will produce a cluster of showy blooms, take a rest, and then bloom again.

Combining several streptocarpus plants creates a profusion of color.

AT A GLANCE
❖
STREPTOCARPUS
Streptocarpus hybridus

Features: vibrant, trumpet-shaped flowers over mounding foliage

Flowering: yes

Colors: blue, violet, red, pink, or white

Height: 10 to 12 inches

Light: bright, indirect

Water: evenly moist

Pests: mealybugs

Remarks: blooms almost year-round

Blooming plants are available in several series of mixed colors. Your best bets are one of the series such as Olympus, Thalia, Windowsill Magic, Royal Mixed, and Nymph, which sport bright, long-lasting color.

The Basics of Care

To keep streptocarpus blooming prolifically, give it winter light from a south-, east-, or west-facing window. In summer, give it bright, indirect light, but keep it out of hot sun. The plant prefers temperatures between 70 and 75 degrees in daytime and 60 to 65 degrees at night. Temperatures above 80 degrees will reduce blooming, and leaves may wilt or scorch.

When streptocarpus is producing new leaves, keep its soil evenly moist and feed monthly with an all-purpose, soluble houseplant fertilizer. It needs a humid atmosphere. (See page 24 for ways to increase humidity.)

This plant does best with a moist, fertile soil and good drainage. Use a premium-quality African violet potting soil.

Easy to propagate. You can start streptocarpus plants by rooting leaf cuttings.

Troubleshooting

Streptocarpus is relatively pest-free, though mealybugs sometimes become a problem. See pages 124–125 for more about this pest.

Many blossoms of streptocarpus have a light dusting of color in their throats.

Streptocarpus works well in decorative containers, such as this brass cachepot.

Wax Plant

The common name wax plant comes from the plant's blossoms, which look as though they are made of paraffin.

Wax plants offer the attractive combination of unusual mounding and trailing foliage coupled with flowers that send out a heavenly fragrance.

Wax plant does not flinch at dry indoor air. It can go years without repotting, and it must reach 18 to 24 inches in length before it can bloom. The fragrant, paraffin-like blossoms for which the plant is named vary from white to a deep shade of pink, depending on the selection. Each blossom is actually a cluster of small flowers that makes a bouquet 1 to 2 inches in diameter.

By keeping a wax plant trimmed, you can display it in a table-top container. But once the vine begins to grow, you will need to allow enough room for the long stems. Put it in a hanging basket, or place it in a raised container or on a pedestal. Sunrooms, porches, and terraces are excellent locations to let the wax plant grow to an impressive length.

Species and Selections

The blossoms of wax plant (*Hoya carnosa*) are perhaps its most extravagant feature, but the foliage of some selections runs a close second. Krinkle Kurl (also called Hindu-rope plant) and Hummel's Compacta are memorable tangles of contorted leaves that twist and fold like fortune cookies. In both selections the leaves are close together, but in Hummel's Compacta the leaves are so compressed that it is almost impossible to see the stem.

AT A GLANCE

❖

WAX PLANT
Hoya carnosa

Features: trailing plant with intensely fragrant flowers

Flowering: yes

Colors: pink flowers, green and variegations of green, white, yellow, pink foliage

Height: trailing

Light: bright indirect

Water: let soil surface dry between thorough waterings

Pests: aphids, mealybugs, scales

Remarks: easy to grow

Hummel's Compacta is easy to identify by its folded, twisted leaves.

The common wax plant is green with leaves that lie open. The foliage of other selections, such as Exotica and Variegata, may be colored with yellow, white, or pink. Rubra is a selection in which the pink is deeper and more prominent. The deepest color and brightest variegation appear when wax plant is grown in bright light, but be careful not to place it in direct sun, as this will bleach the leaves to a dull yellow.

The Basics of Care

Give wax plant plenty of bright, indirect light. It does just fine with indoor temperatures of 65 to 75 degrees and average humidity levels. Water when the surface of the soil feels dry; in winter, water just enough to keep the leaves from shriveling. This dry period helps flowering. A healthy plant will bloom at least once in the spring and may continue blooming through the warm months. It may be two to three weeks after buds become visible before they open. After about a week in full bloom, the flowers turn brown, but you need to leave the short stem in place; the flowers will fall off in a couple of days and the stem may bloom again.

Fertilize every other month with an all-purpose, soluble houseplant fertilizer. Wax plant can go outside for the warm spring, summer, and fall months. It can also remain outside longer than many houseplants, as it can withstand temperatures as low as 40 degrees without damage.

Wax plant is usually sold in pots or hanging baskets where the trailing stems spill freely over the edge. These wiry, leafless stems may grow 8 feet long or more, but can be controlled by cutting. Unlike many vines, wax plant will branch wherever it is cut. Pruning all the way back will make the plant fuller. You can also train the vines to climb a wooden support.

Easy to propagate. Start new wax plants by rooting cuttings taken from mature stems, not from tender new growth.

Troubleshooting

Rinsing the plant every two to three weeks helps keep it free of pests. Mealybugs are especially difficult to control once they are protected by the folds of the Hindu-rope selection. Aphids and scales also attack wax plant. See pages 124–125 for more about these pests.

Exotica offers stunning multicolored foliage.

This young Variegata is ideal for filling a broad, low space.

Pests and Diseases

By carefully inspecting plants before you buy, caring for them properly, and inspecting them again before you move them indoors after the summer, you can avoid or minimize the risk of infestation and disease. If you spot a problem, isolate the affected plant as soon as possible to keep it from spreading.

Pesticides can help fight these problems, but recommendations for using them change frequently. For information on specific pesticides, contact your local Extension Service office. Before using strong pesticides, try milder treatments such as insecticidal soap and highly refined horticultural oil. Always follow label directions for safely applying and storing pesticides.

Aphids

Aphids are tiny, pear-shaped insects that are ⅛ to ¼ inch long; the types that attach to houseplants are frequently green, clear, or white. They suck sap from the tender young stems and flower buds, causing curled leaves, misshapen growth, and unopened buds. Aphids produce hundreds of offspring in a few weeks, so it is crucial to control them as soon as they appear.

Crown and Root Rot

Overwatering leaves plants vulnerable to a fungus that can rot their roots and crown. Stems at the top of plants like African violet become soft and mushy when affected by crown rot. Affected roots become brown and soft, and the plant wilts because it cannot absorb water. To avoid the problem, water properly. Once rot sets in, it is difficult to stop, and you may eventually need to replace the plant.

Leaf Spot

Dry soil, high temperatures, fluoride toxicity, and insect damage can cause spots on leaves, as can bacterial and fungal infections. Careful diagnosis is essential to proper treatment.

Spots caused by a fungus may be reddish, brown, or black, and sometimes are bordered by a ring.

Remove any infected leaves and spray with a recommended fungicide.

Bacterial leaf spot produces soft, water-soaked lesions on leaves. The spots are often brown with a yellow ring around them, and they sometimes produce an unpleasant odor. Bacterial leaf spot is difficult to control. Isolate the affected plants and remove infected foliage. Wash your hands and clean tools carefully to avoid spreading the disease. If the disease continues to spread, discard the plant.

Mealybugs

Mealybugs are soft-bodied insects that are about ¼ inch long and that are covered with a white, cottony-looking wax. Some species have three tail-like projections. They suck sap from tender young leaves and stems, causing deformed foliage. They may attack African violet, cactus, citrus, gloxinia, jade plant, palm, and schefflera.

Treat affected plants quickly; heavy infestations can kill them. Use rubbing alcohol on a paper towel to physically remove large cottony masses; the wax from insecticides often protects eggs and newly hatched mealybugs. Spray the plant thoroughly with a recommended pesticide.

Powdery Mildew

Powdery mildew looks like a white or gray dusting on the surface of the leaves. It is most likely to appear on plants growing outdoors or in a greenhouse. While it is unlikely to develop in an air-conditioned home, begonias and kalanchoes are particularly susceptible.

Powdery mildew weakens the plant by causing leaves to dry and wither. To control it, give plants plenty of room; good air circulation is important to keep the foliage dry. Once the disease appears, it is difficult to control. Spray with a recommended fungicide.

Scales

Scales are soft- or hard-bodied insects that cling to the underside of leaves and along stems. The hard-bodied types look like tiny raised surfaces on the leaf or stem and can be scraped away with a fingernail. The soft-bodied scales do not have this covering but may be covered in white wax or a mass of cottonlike fibers. Scales attack ferns and many other houseplants; however, you must examine fern fronds carefully because scales can look like fern spores on the back of the fertile fronds.

Control scales when they first appear, as they are difficult to kill when their numbers increase. Scales can produce dozens of eggs, so spray often to kill the crawlers, or young scales, as they hatch and crawl away. Systemic insecticides offer the best control.

Spider Mites

Spider mites are tiny, spiderlike insects that collect on the underside of leaves and on flower and leaf buds. They suck sap from the plants, causing deformed leaves and unopened buds. Central heating creates perfect conditions for their growth in the winter, so be especially watchful then. Spider mites seem to prefer cactus, croton, cyclamen, palm, and schefflera but will attack almost any houseplant. You may not see spider mites until their feeding begins to make the topside of the leaves look faded and mottled. Turning a leaf over will reveal clusters of pinpoint-sized spider mites and often their delicate webbing. Use a magnifying glass to be sure.

The best way to prevent spider mites is to give houseplants a shower every week or two, making sure to wash the underside of the leaves. It is important to control a serious infestation, as spider mites multiply quickly. To kill spider mites, thoroughly coat the underside of leaves with a recommended insecticide. In severe cases, you may have to discard the plant.

Thrips

Thrips are tiny, brown or black torpedo-shaped insects that hide in the petals of flowers and folds of leaves. They feed on African violets and other flowering plants and are especially attracted to white or light-colored flowers. They suck sap, causing brown, withered flowers and scarred, distorted leaves. They can also cause citrus to drop blossoms early and produce deformed fruit. To discourage thrips, spray plants with a recommended insecticide.

Whiteflies

These white, mothlike insects are only ⅛ inch long and are found on the underside of leaves, sucking sap and leaving foliage yellowed and spotted. If you shake the plant, they will fly out, but then they will light again. Whiteflies are particularly troublesome in greenhouses and can be found on many plants, including azaleas and begonias. To control whiteflies, spray the underside of leaves with a recommended pesticide.

Index

Index

Special Thanks

John O'Hagan, photographs, 88, 89, 91, 98, 105, 108, 112

Southern Progress Corpation Library Staff